Cultural Revolution

Posters & Memorabilia

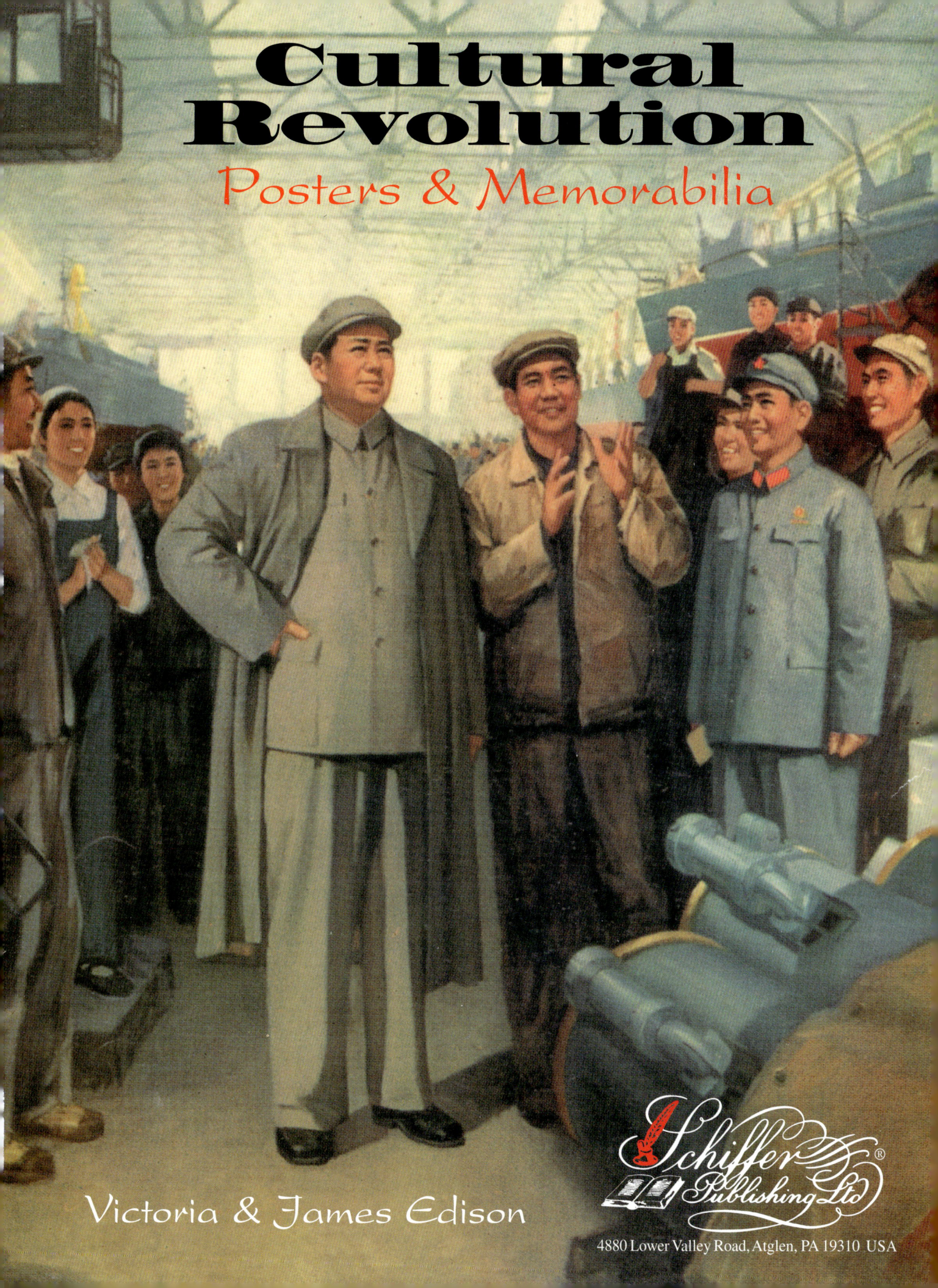

Victoria & James Edison

Schiffer Publishing Ltd

4880 Lower Valley Road, Atglen, PA 19310 USA

Dedication

To our daughter, our parents and our grandparents.

Acknowledgments

We would like to thank Stefan Landsberger, whose aid was invaluable in understanding the Cultural Revolution and its many nuances, who guided us toward many valuable third-party sources and provided key edits to add the necessary finishing touches to the book. Joseph Liu provided information on the use and meaning of the political references and details about the Cultural Revolution that were not always known to the Western world. Tracy Kunichika, who spent her valuable vacation hours away from the non-profit organization she runs in India taking many supplemental photos that fill this book.

Last, and most of all, we would like to thank our family, especially our parents, who encouraged us to pursue our passions and gave us the tools to write and think, and the support to follow our dreams.

Library of Congress Cataloging-in-Publication Data

Edison, Victoria.
  Cultural revolution : posters & memorabilia / Victoria & James Edison.
    p. cm.
  Includes bibliographical references (p.191)
  ISBN: 0-7643-2236-2 (hardcover)
1. China—History—Cultural Revolutioin, 1966-1976—Posters. I. Edison, James. II. Title.

DS778.7.E35 2006
951.05'6—dec22

2005020547

Cover and book designed by Bruce Waters
Type set in Korinna BT/Goudy Oldstyle

ISBN: 0-7643-2236-2
Printed in China
1 2 3 4

Disclaimer

Published by Schiffer Publishing Ltd.
4880 Lower Valley Road
Atglen, PA 19310
Phone: (610) 593-1777; Fax: (610) 593-2002
E-mail: Info@schifferbooks.com

For the largest selection of fine reference books on this and related subjects, please visit our web site at
www.schifferbooks.com
We are always looking for people to write books on new and related subjects. If you have an idea for a book please contact us at the above address.

This book may be purchased from the publisher.
Include $3.95 for shipping.
Please try your bookstore first.
You may write for a free catalog.

In Europe, Schiffer books are distributed by
Bushwood Books
6 Marksbury Ave.
Kew Gardens
Surrey TW9 4JF England
Phone: 44 (0) 20 8392-8585; Fax: 44 (0) 20 8392-9876
E-mail: info@bushwoodbooks.co.uk
Free postage in the U.K., Europe; air mail at cost.

Contents

Preface

Stefan Landsberger

Politics can be high drama, and one of the most dramatic political events in the history of the People's Republic of China (PRC) undoubtedly was the Cultural Revolution that engulfed the nation from 1966 to 1976. The drama of the era not only touched the millions of people who suddenly saw themselves prosecuted in the often bewildering mass movements that were aimed at weeding out a host of "enemies of the state," but also characterized many elements of the process of political communications between the leadership and the people.

There is probably no other political system that has made such overwhelming and enthusiastic use of propaganda art as the one that is in place in China. Even before the founding of the PRC in 1949, when the Chinese Communist Party (CCP) was in hiding in Yan'an in the remote regions of northwest China and struggling for its survival, great energy was invested in ways to reach the largely illiterate population. Many of the artists who sympathized with the Party were engaged in composing rousing revolutionary songs, organizing and designing theatre skits, drawing comic strips, painting inspirational murals, and writing stories about heroic Party members and the great changes that were taking place in the areas that already had been "liberated." The CCP used many mechanisms that had proven their worth in the preceding centuries, such as model emulation. But non-native cultural elements that had been tried out earlier and with success by the Communist Party of the Soviet Union were also introduced, most notably the leader portrait as part of a much broader cult of leader worship.

After 1949, propaganda art was employed as one of the major means to provide examples of correct behavior. It made concrete the many different abstract policies and grandiose visions of the future under CCP-rule. With the high rate of illiteracy in China during the 1940s and 1950s, the visualization of abstract ideas worked especially well to educate the people. One artistic expression of propaganda, the poster, could be produced cheaply and easily, and this made it a greatly favored vehicle for political communication. Widely available, posters could be seen everywhere and provided an excellent way to bring some color to the otherwise drab surroundings where the people lived. Posters were able to penetrate even the lowest levels of social organization and cohabitation: the multicolored posters could be seen adorning the walls not only of offices and factories, but of houses and dormitories as well. Most people liked the posters for their colors, composition, and visual contents, and did not pay too much attention to the slogans printed underneath.

The years of the great mass movements, such as the Great Leap Forward (1958-1960) and the subsequent Cultural Revolution (1966-1976), when millions of people were mobilized into action, saw the climax in propaganda art production. The posters reached their peak of artistic expression, both in form and content. Particularly during the Cultural Revolution, politics increasingly took precedence over any other subject in propaganda posters. Chairman Mao Zedong, as the Great Teacher, the Great Leader, the Great Helmsman, and the Supreme Commander, seemed to have become the only permissible subject of the era. His face was usually painted in red and other warm tones, and in such a way that it appeared smooth and seemed to radiate as the primary source of light in a composition, illuminating the faces of the people around him. His countenance beamed down from the many huge billboards located along the streets and avenues in China's urban areas. His portrait decorated steam engines and harbor cranes. Photographs showing his face were placed in the fields, where they oversaw all aspects of rural production. The people themselves wore Mao badges in varying sizes pinned to their chests.

The quotations from his writings, urging people to behave and think in a way he approved, were often compared to a magical or supernatural weapon (a "demon-exposing mirror"), a "spiritual atom bomb" or even a "beacon light" The *Red Book* was distributed in millions and millions of copies; the Mao-quotes were studied, chanted, sung, and used as magic spells.

In the summer of 1966, the first "big character posters" were pasted on walls, in which so-called anti-Party elements, real or perceived enemies of Mao, were attacked. Intellectuals, leaders, and artists were persecuted, and schools and universities were closed to give students the opportunity to follow Mao's call for continuous revolution by becoming Red Guards. Waves of criticism engulfed the country, and practically every official was accused. By 1968, this struggle had escalated into a veritable civil war. The country and the economy were in a shambles. Life in China in those years was definitely unpleasant, but none of this can be seen in the propaganda of the period.

Many of the posters produced in the early phases of the Cultural Revolution clearly were made for local purposes. The victims shown on these extremely aggressive images were often local luminaries who are being pierced by pens and writing brushes wielded by Red Guards or the angry masses of soldiers-workers-peasants, or beaten with hammers and cudgels. With their black, red, and white coloring, which is unique for this period, they give the impression of having been produced as block prints. But even posters of this type were published and distributed by departments at the central level. And as in other cases, it has become clear that even for these "spontaneous," "local" posters, the central levels provided the examples.

Much of the propaganda art of the Cultural Revolution was shaped by the ideas and dictates of Mao's wife Jiang Qing. This contributed greatly to the dramatic quality of Chinese propaganda in the 1960s and 1970s. Using the arts as a platform, she succeeded in clawing her way to the top, exacting revenge from her personal enemies in the process. Instrumental in this was her close cooperation with the People's Liberation Army, headed by Lin Biao. Under her leadership, certain theatrical conventions that had been introduced in her so-called revolutionary model works made their way into almost all other types of art. Thanks to Jiang's ideas about the ideal representation of heroic and villainous characters, the "Three Prominences," heroes had to be *gao* (lofty), *da* (glorious), and *quan* (complete), while the villains had to be base, shabby, ugly, and stupid. The central characters were portrayed realistically and were always in the center of the action, flooded with light from the sun or from hidden sources,

just as if they were on stage. Moreover, when looking at the propaganda posters of the period, it really seems as if we, the spectators, are looking upward, as if the action is indeed taking place upon a stage. The same theatricality is also evident in the ceramic statuettes, even the ones that are not directly inspired by scenes from Jiang's model works.

Propaganda art slowly but surely disappeared after the end of the Cultural Revolution. The rise of Deng Xiaoping after 1978 and his policies, which shifted the focus from politics to economic reform and development, and stressed getting rich instead of becoming a pure revolutionary, contributed to the demise of the genre as well. The Cultural Revolution was officially declared to have been a "lost decade," or as "ten years of turmoil."

Ironically, though, as reform policies, social upheavals, and dislocation changed the shape and rhythm of China, the revolutionary era increasingly was looked upon with a mixture of nostalgia for an imaginary golden past and yearning for the more orderly society that only existed in the people's imagination. True, times often had been bad, there had been a famine, personal futures had been uncertain, but at least everybody was in it together and had shared the same fate. Banking on this reinterpretation of the past, the centenary of Mao's birth was marked (and marketed) by the CCP with a flood of memorabilia and kitsch. When this "Mao Fever" cooled down after 1993, Mao memorabilia remained available, although mainly in the larger urban centers. By then, Chinese customer interest seemed to have waned or shifted to other subjects. Foreigners working in or passing through China, however, continued to be fascinated by Cultural Revolution kitsch and Mao trinkets. As a result, illegal copies and reprints of Cultural Revolution propaganda materials, often of inferior quality, started to appear on the market.

The net effects of the three decades of high revolution on the Chinese population are widespread distrust and apathy towards politics. Hardly anybody cares about who is in or out in Zhongnanhai, the centre of the Chinese political system. Urbanites all seem to be dreaming of earning an MBA at a Western university, going into business, and becoming rich. People from the countryside flock to the cities, hoping they can profit somewhere at the margins of the emerging urban consumer culture. Propaganda art has disappeared completely and has been replaced by its more up-market sibling, commercial advertising.

And yet, a new interest in these forceful political expressions of the past seems to be emerging. Jiang Qing's model works are still very much appreciated today. Songbooks and VCDs or DVDs of the model operas are readily available and quite popular with the many people who were introduced to them – and probably bored to tears by them – more than 35 years ago. The arias are often sung in karaoke bars and at parties. And during a soccer match between Chinese and Japanese teams in the summer of 2004, Chinese spectators in the stands held up reproductions of posters from the

Cultural Revolution to support their favorites. Although the slogans had been adapted to the event at hand, the images seemed to be as rousing as they had before.

Victoria Edison's book introduces many of the materials that were produced during the Cultural Revolution. They range from posters to articles of clothing, from Red Books to Mao badges, from statuettes to ration coupons. All artifacts are part of the political drama that swept over China. All have a story to tell, although some are invested with more poignant personal memories of the events that took place. They shed light on the extraordinarily dramatic era that preceded China's reintegration with the world.

Introduction:

A Bygone Era

The earliest memory I have about my childhood was with my paternal grandparents. Having been sent to the "May 7 Cadre" camp to be re-educated, they returned from four years of hard labor just in time to welcome the arrival of their first granddaughter. Shortly after I was born, my mother, a high school teacher, had to take her students down to the countryside to farm the rice fields with the peasants. My father, a "reformed" engineer turned into a writer for the Revolutionary Committee of his factory work unit, was ordered to work late every evening to come up with the next Big Character Poster for the next day's political study. They left me with my grandparents.

Fortunately, my grandparents were largely left in peace after their release and were only required to gather with other senior May 7 Cadre members in regular struggle sessions. They did not suffer the fate of so many others at the hands of Red Guards. As a result they had plenty of time to dote on their granddaughter, me. Our days would start with a stroll to the park, about an hour's walk from home. We would come back with seeds found in the park and would tend the small garden in front of our house. We raised little chickens and I had a pet turtle. In the evening we listened to short wave radio programs. My grandfather kept the volume down, so low that we could barely hear. Only when I was older did I understand that we were listening to the Voice of America, a criminal act in 1970s China. Anyone caught listening would be labeled a "Counter Revolutionary" and thrown in jail. My grandparents took me with them to their struggle and self-criticism sessions. The first words I spoke were "Revolutionary Committee (*Ge Wei Hui*)," something they said often, typically with fear in their voice.

The happiness of my early years was shattered by the disappearance of my mother. She left and nobody would explain to me why or how it happened. She even-tually returned, but only when I was an adult did I learn what had happened. The government had arrested her for criticizing a government leader, and she faced the death penalty. My father took me to his home province in the north and I spent a few weeks with his relatives while he worked on getting my mother out of jail. Fortunately, the Revolutionary Committee member in charge of my mother's case had been my father's teacher in elementary school and was very fond of him. With the teacher's intercession, the government released my mother. The accusation remained on her permanent record (*Dang An*). Her crime, I later learned, was that she told a close friend of hers that Hua Guofeng (Mao's designated successor) lacked the charisma to be the leader of China. She cited as example that he picked his nose repeatedly during a tele-vised speech to foreign leaders. Her close friend took the opportunity to report her to promote her own po-sition.

Like many children who were born into the Cul-tural Revolution, my childhood was filled with ideol-ogy. Lei Feng's self-sacrificing spirit dominated the way I behaved and thought. This changed, however, after I moved to a special economic zone in the south in the mid-1980s. As part of the economic modernization pro-gram, Deng Xiaoping designated special areas where capitalist economic activities could take place. These places grew explosively as money from Hong Kong and overseas Chinese businessmen flooded in to take ad-vantage of the cheap and plentiful labor. Former fish-ing villages such as Shenzhen and Zhuhai sprouted fac-tories and modern high-rise apartments. The difference between this new world and what I had known in Hunan was a shock, and my adjustment was difficult. In addition to economic and cultural differences, the people there spoke an entirely different dialect, Cantonese. I turned inward, reading and writing in order to understand the changing world better. The stories of struggle in the "scar literature" of the time made more sense to me than my fellow classmates' fashionable attire and summer vacation spots. By the time I returned from the U.S. in 1992, China had changed so radically that I no longer recognized most of the places I had known. No one wanted to talk about the Cultural Revolution and no one wanted to talk about anything related to Communism. The word "money" came up constantly. People were excited about the future and no one bothered to talk about the past.

Because the time I spent in China was so limited, collecting Chinese political memorabilia became a way for me to reconnect to my childhood. By capturing a bygone era that most Chinese people desperately want to escape and forget, I became closer to the country I had left behind. Every evening when I sing lullabies to my own daughter, born in the United States, I am reminded how lucky we are.

Chinese Lullaby from the Cultural Revolution -

"Little Swallow"

Little swallow wears colorful clothes,
Every spring you come to visit us,
I ask little swallow "why you are visiting us?"
Little swallow says "because the spring is so beautiful here."

Little swallow, let me tell you,
Next year we will have an even better spring,
We are building a factory, and installing new machines,
I hope you come to visit us every year.

Chapter 1
Bombard the Headquarters

For many who remember the Great Proletarian Cultural Revolution, the defining moment was the posting of Mao's huge banner (often called a big character poster[1]) in August 1966 exhorting his Red Guards to "Bombard the Headquarters." Although this was not the start of many of the institutions and practices that are identified with the Cultural Revolution, such as the Red Guards, struggle sessions, and denunciations of authority figures, it marked a shift to a new phase. It signaled that something truly revolutionary was about to happen, a challenge to the authority of the central government.

The attack was a long time coming. Mao and his top followers had organized into the Cultural Revolution group under the leadership of the Central Committee. According to his sixteen-point decision, "the cultural and educational units and leading organs of the Party and government in the large and medium cities are the points of concentration of the present proletarian cultural revolution." The decision also identified rightist and reactionary bourgeois scholars as the targets of the movement. But the decision stated unequivocally that "the main target of the present movement is those within the Party who are in authority and are taking the capitalist road."

Mao's main target was none other than Liu Shaoqi, his heir apparent. Liu Shaoqi's criticism of Mao's Great Leap Forward campaign, along with a variety of other disagreements, made him a thorn in Mao's side. Mao's first big character poster, which was published during the Eleventh Plenum, was a direct attack on Liu Shaoqi and Deng Xiaoping for their capitalist ways.[2] With the Red Guards ready to march forward on Mao's command, China launched a countrywide campaign against capitalists and other class enemies. Senior officials of the Chinese central government were removed from their positions and forced into early retirement (at best), and often suffered humiliation, abuse, or even death. Liu Shaoqi died in prison in 1969.

Bombard the Headquarters – My First Big Character Wall Poster. Depicting Red Guards who are *Beijing Daxue* (Beijing University, or "*beida*") students holding signs reading "Revolution is Not a Crime" and "To Rebel is Justified." Mao's words appeared in an essay titled "My First Big Character Wall Poster," which launched the Cultural Revolution by mobilizing youth around the country. The First Big Character Wall Poster (*da zi bao*) was posted by a group of radical professors in Beijing University on May 25, 1966. Ceramic statue. c.1968. 12" x 8" x 18". $200 - $400

The most infamous poster of the era was developed by the son of the Chinese historian Jian Bozan. A radical student from the Central Art Academy, he created a poster depicting a number of senior party cadres, including Liu Shaoqi and Deng Xiaoping. Although his intention was to follow Mao's direction, his bluntness was viewed as making fun of the Chinese Communist Party and the Cultural Revolution. He was arrested shortly after and was imprisoned. Despite this, Mao's targets were indeed depicted in the poster.

Group Ugliness Poster. Well known poster depicting fallen communist leaders, such as Liu Shaoqi and Deng Xiaoping. One of the best depictions of prominent Chinese Communist Party (CCP) leaders who had fallen out of favor, with their names and pictures. The artist is the son of the famous Chinese historian Jian Bozan. Print on paper. 1967. 15" x 21". $300 - $500

Bombard the Headquarters. People's Police Protection Unit of Mao Zedong Revolution Rebellion Group. Wood block print on paper. $60 - $80

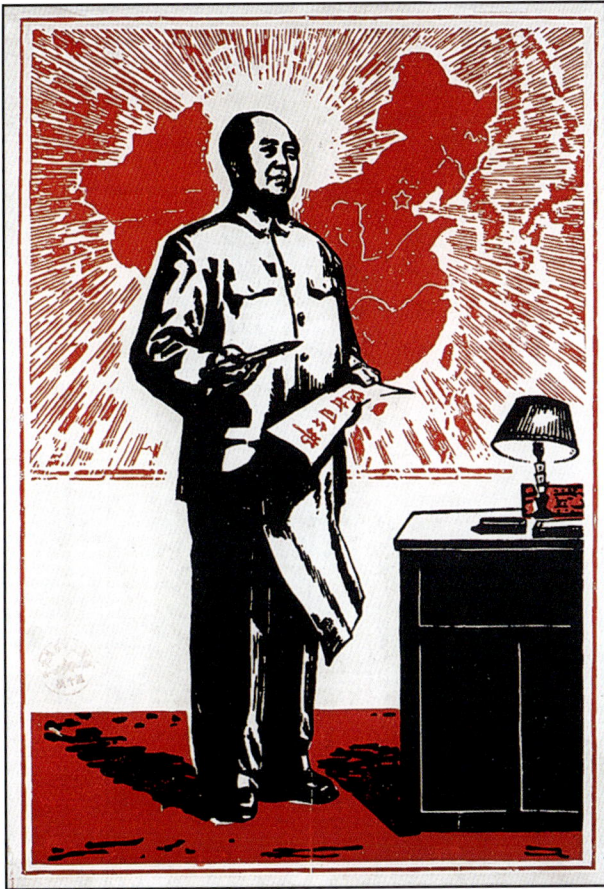

Bombard the Headquarters. Central Fine Art University Fight Team. Wood block print on paper. $60 - $80

Down with Liu Shaoqi - Conduct Revolution Great Criticism. Wood block print on paper. $80 - $120

Chapter 2
The Cultural
Revolution Group

If the big character poster "Bombard the Head-quarters" is viewed as a seminal event in the start of the Cultural Revolution, it is the formation of the original Cultural Revolution Group that prepared the central government for the movement. The original group consisted of five men, led by Kang Sheng, who supported Mao. The other four members actually opposed Mao and his previous policies.

无产阶级文化大革命，实质上是在社会主义条件下，无产阶级反对资产阶级和一切剥削阶级的政治大革命，是中国共产党及其领导下的广大革命人民群众和国民党反动派长期斗争的继续，是无产阶级和资产阶级阶级斗争的继续。 毛泽东

热烈欢呼湖南省革命委员会成立 一九六八年四月十日

The Great Proletarian Cultural Revolution is in essence, under the socialist society's condition, a large political revolution conducted by the great proletarian class against capitalist class and other exploiting classes, a long continuation of the struggle conducted by the Masses of the People against the Nationalist Party's Counterrevolutionaries led by the Chinese Communist Party, and the continuation of struggle between the Great Proletarian class and the Capitalist class. Image of Mao Zedong, Lin Biao, Zhou Enlai, Chen Boda, Kang Sheng and Jiang Qing (Madam Mao), key figures in the Cultural Revolution. Background shown is Tiananmen and the Forbidden City. Published to celebrate the establishment of the Hunan Revolutionary Committee. Hunan Revolutionary Committee, April 10, 1968. Print on paper. Print run 665,000, 0.18 Yuan. $150 - $300

We will forever be loyal to our dear beloved Chairman Mao. Featured figures are Mao Zedong, Lin Biao, Jiang Qing, Kang Sheng, Chen Boda, and Zhou Enlai, who were major participants in the Cultural Revolution. Kunming Workers' Art United Fighting Group. Print on paper. 27" x 13.5". $150 - $300

Celebration of the 18th anniversary of People's Republic of China, follow Chairman's footstep to revolution. Photos shown are Mao, Lin Biao, Jiang Qing, Kang Sheng, Chen Boda, and Zhou Enlai standing atop Tiananmen. They were the early and major players of the Cultural Revolution. Jointly created by East Wind Printing Company Workers Revolution Rebel Team, Shanghai People's Art Publishing House Rebel Team, Shanghai # 58 Middle School, East is Red People's Commune, and Capital City Red Representation Team Central Art School. Print on paper. c.1967. $150 - $300

The New Cultural Revolution Group, formed on May 28, 1966, was dominated by Mao's supporters and the radical intellectuals surrounding Jiang Qing, Mao's wife, otherwise known as Madam Mao. They reported directly to Mao, and not to the Party Secretariat, which was mainly staffed by Liu Shaoqi's and Deng Xiaoping's followers. The new group was headed by Chen Boda, with Kang Sheng and Zhou Enlai as advisers. Other key members included Jiang Qing, Zhang Chunqiao, and Yao Wenyuan. With this new group in charge of the Cultural Revolution, Mao gained the ability to attack and undermine or remove people he suspected of opposing him.

Chapter 3
Rise of Lin Biao, Mao's Heir

With Liu Shaoqi out of the picture, Lin Biao became Mao's heir apparent. A general from the Northeastern Army, Lin Biao had been in the Anti-Japan war military school in Yanan with Mao Zedong and was head of the PLA. Although he did not coin it, Lin Biao extolled the "four greats" of Mao, "great leader, great teacher, great general, great helmsman," and promoted Mao worship in the country. He organized the military to print volumes of Mao's quotations in Red Books. His apparent loyalty to Mao made him an instant favorite to succeed Mao. His position as Mao's heir was confirmed at the 9th Party Congress in April 1969.

Lin Biao's military career started at an early age. Lin joined the communist youth corps in 1925 and later studied at the Huangpu (Whampoa) military academy, where he met Zhou Enlai, who later became Premier of China. Most of the Chinese army commanders during both the civil war and the Sino-Japanese war came from Whampoa, China's West Point. Lin fought under Zhu De and met Mao in 1928 in Jinggangshan. Lin Biao was very active during the Long March and led the capture of the Luding Bridge, a key turning point in the Chinese civil war. Lin was also responsible for defeating the Nationalist army in Manchuria, Beijing, and Tianjin. In 1959, Lin replaced Peng Dehuai as Defense Minister. He was considered a military genius and used his fame and skills to promote himself as Mao's heir. In this effort he encouraged the Cult of Mao, distributing Red Books and allying himself with Madam Mao and the Gang of the Four. From 1967 to 1971, a large amount of memorabilia was created promoting Mao and Lin Biao together, reinforcing and demonstrating Lin's position. No one else was displayed so prominently with Mao. The image of Mao and Lin in front of Tiananmen reviewing the Red Guards appeared on millions of ceramic items, including mugs, plaques, plates and statues.

Although Lin was called Mao's closest comrade in arms and officially designated as Mao's successor, Mao started to have second thoughts. These doubts intensified as Mao became aware of Lin's independent power base in the PLA, and Mao began to withdraw his support for some of Lin's close associates. Seeing his people falling out of favor with Mao, Lin sensed a threat to his position. He and his faction met to stage a coup, code named "571" (a pun in Chinese on the word for "armed uprising"), led by his son Lin Liguo, who was in charge of the air force. Unfortunately for Lin, Mao found out about the coup. The plot exposed, Lin and his family attempted to flee to the Soviet Union, but their plane crashed in Mongolia, killing all aboard. The description above is the official version of events, but it should be noted that there are other versions of the events leading up to Lin's death.

Establish Mao's Theory's as Definite Authority. Lin Biao holding Mao's book titled "Serve the People, In Memory of Bai Qiu'en (Dr. Norman Bethune)." Central Fine Art School Revolutionary Red Flag Group, c 1969. Wood block print on paper. $60 - $80

Mao Zedong and Lin Biao in a "Red Flag" jeep reviewing the Cultural Revolution Army. Mao reviewed millions of Red Guards at Tiananmen Square in mass rallies from 1966 to 1968. Red Guards converged on Beijing from all over the country, encouraged by free transport and room and board. Ceramic statue. 15.5" x 9" x 12". $200 - $400

The truth about Lin came out gradually in subsequent years, both from official sources and folklore that circulated among the population. His death in a plane crash was suspicious, and even at the time some said that the Chinese Air Force shot down his plane over Mongolia. Others speculated that the pilot was not aware of the escape plan and, upon realizing Lin's purpose, refused to comply. It was said that the pilot had a gunshot wound to the head, leading people to speculate that he was shot during an inflight struggle and, after his death, no one was able to pilot the plane. The official story from the Chinese government was that the plane ran out of fuel. Recently uncovered information, however, suggests that there was significant fuel at the crash site, suggesting that the plane did not crash for lack of fuel.

My paternal grandfather joined Lin Biao's Northeastern army in the 1930s, and has his own opinion of Lin Biao. According to him, Lin was one of the least corrupt army officials. Lin was a quiet man who kept to himself and didn't drink or gamble, even after battles when most of the soldiers celebrated their victories and toasted comrades. Lin made sure that his soldiers were taken care of, though he didn't mix with them.

In 1992, while visiting China for the first time after the Tiananmen Square incident in 1989, I met a young Beijing University (*BeiDa*) student who was selling Chinese Propaganda posters in a flea market. Among them was a poster showing Mao, Lin, and Zhou Enlai. Not realizing that I was fluent in Chinese, he spoke in broken English to me. Pointing at Mao and Zhou, he said, "Bad," and then pointing to Lin, he said "Good." He then looked at me, presumably expecting a shocked reaction. He got one; I hadn't realized that others shared my grandfather's view of Lin Biao. I was interested in finding out how he had formed that impression, given that the government still officially considered Lin a traitor. I asked him in English, "Why?" He merely shrugged, unwilling or unable to explain it to me.

Along the lines suggested by this, the public opinion of Lin appears to have shifted over the years, and the government has grown softer in its criticism. At the same time, the government's defense of Mao has become less strident, admitting certain mistakes but reiterating his central role in the emancipation of China from the imperial Western powers. Lin's plot against Mao in this context appears less traitorous and his image has been to a great extent rehabilitated. Recent books about Lin and his role in China once more emphasize his key role in the formation of the People's Republic of China, characterizing him as a military genius.

Pi Lin Pi Kong (Criticize Lin Biao criticize Confucius campaign). On January 18, 1974, a document prepared under the direction of Jiang Qing entitled "The doctrines of Lin Biao, Confucius and Mencius" was circulated in the Central Government. Originated with a comment by Mao to a Qinghua University study group in August 1973, *Pi Kong* was an effort to criticize China's senior intellectual and writer Guo Moro for praising the Confucians and condemning China's First Emperor, Qin Shi Huang, known as a suppressor and tormentor of intellectuals and people. Ironically, his countrymen compared Mao to Qin Shi Huang. At the same time, *Pi Kong* was also directed against Zhou Enlai, who was considered to be a modern-day Confucius. *Pi Lin* was a movement aimed to criticize Lin Biao after his death. Used as elementary educational material depicting young pioneers' effort in the *Pi Lin Pi Pong* campaign. Print on Paper. $60 - $100

Mao's heart and our hearts are together. 7th inspection of the Cultural Revolution Army. Movie poster. Central News and Documentary Production Company and August First Movie Company. Print on paper. 29" by 21". $60 - $80

Glorious example, great new creation. Chairman Mao's 8th inspection of the Cultural Revolution army. Lin Biao standing next to Chairman Mao. Central News and Documentary Movie Company and August First Movie Company. Published by China Movie Distribution Company. Print on paper. 30" x 21" $60 - $80

Success belongs to us. Mao Zedong and Lin Biao. Wood block print. Printed in celebration of CCP 8th plenum 12th Central Committee meeting. Sichuan People's Publishing House, November 1968. Wood block print on paper. 0.10 Yuan. 30 x 21 $60 - $80

Mao Zedong and Lin Biao reviewing Red Guards in Tiananmen Square. Ceramic statue. c.1968 12" x 3" x 12". $100 - $200

Mao Zedong's Talk re: Serve the People and Lin Biao's Words on the Three Much-Read Articles (*lao san pian*). The Three Much-Read Articles are: Serve the People, In Memory of Bai Qiu'en (Dr. Norman Bethune), and Yu Gong Moving the Mountain. These three articles were printed in many millions of copies during Cultural Revolution and intended to serve as a guide for correct revolutionary thought and behavior. People's Art Publishing house, June 1968. Print on paper. 0.16 Yuan. $60 - $80

Our Great Leader Chairman Mao and his close comrade Lin Biao at Zhongnanhai. People's Publishing House, Henan, December 1967. Print on paper. 0.16 Yuan. $60 - $80

Long long live Chairman Mao! Great Leader Chairman Mao and his close Comrade Lin Biao at the Ninth Plenum of the Chinese Communist Party Central Committee's First Meeting. Poster marking the Ninth Plenum, a landmark meeting in which Lin Biao was appointed as Mao Zedong's successor and the Cultural Revolution officially declared to have ended. People's Publishing House, c.1969. Print on paper. 0.28 Yuan. $60 - $80

Lin Biao holding a Red Book. Lin Biao rose to power during the Cultural Revolution and replaced Liu Shaoqi as second-in-command and Mao's heir apparent. Criticized by Mao as an ultra-rightist. Died on September 13, 1971, in a plane crash while attempting to flee to the Soviet Union (September 13 Incident). Was subsequently declared a traitor. Ceramic statue. c.1968 11"x 4" x 3". $40 - $60

Mao Zedong, Lin Biao and Jiang Qing. Three most influential players in the Cultural Revolution. Lin, vice chairman, Mao's formal heir apparent died later in plane crash. Jiang Qing, leader of the Gang of Four, declared a traitor and sentenced to life in prison. She died in her residence on May 14, 1991, allegedly by suicide. Ceramic statue. c.1969-1976. 16" x 12" x 10". $90- $200

Lin Biao and Jiang Qing. Ceramic statue. c.1968. 10" x 14". $90- $200

Long Live and success to Chairman Mao's Revolutionary Road. Mao Zedong and Lin Biao propaganda pictorial booklet, used to prepare and promote Lin's succession to Mao. Chinese People's Liberation Army Navy Propaganda Art Department workers. It is illustrated here on pages 20 through 27. Shandong People's Publishing House, June 1971. 0.70 Yuan. $80 - $200 for the set

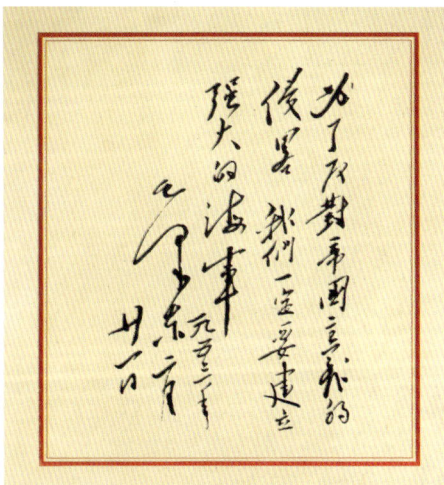

In order to prevent imperialist invasion, we must establish a strong naval force. Mao Zedong. Print on paper. 1953.

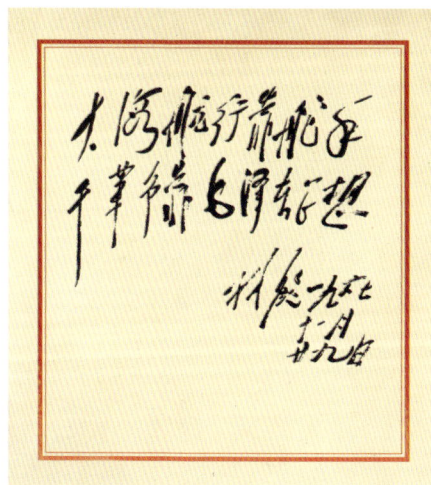

Sailing the seas depends on a helmsman. Waging revolution relies on Mao's Thoughts. Lin Biao. Print on paper. 1967.

伟大统帅指方向
伟大领袖毛主席于一九五〇年为《人民海军》杂志创刊号题词

Great General provides direction. Print on paper.

亲切的教导
伟大领袖毛主席于一九五二年二月十四日视察海军领导机关

Warm Teaching. Print on paper.

伟大领袖毛主席在军舰上

Great Leader Chairman Mao inspecting a
Chinese Navy ship. Print on paper.

幸　福　的　航　程

伟大领袖毛主席于一九五三年二月十九日至二十四日
首次视察海军舰艇部队，和海军战士在一起航行四天三夜

Happy Journey. Print on paper.

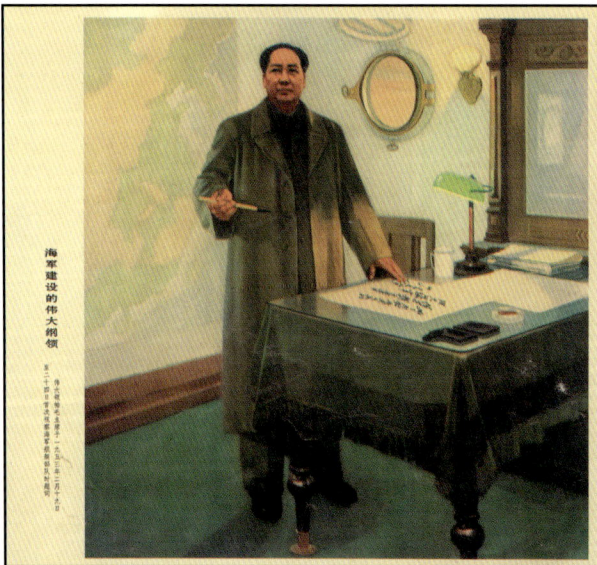

海军建设的伟大纲领

The great direction for the building of the navy. Print on paper.

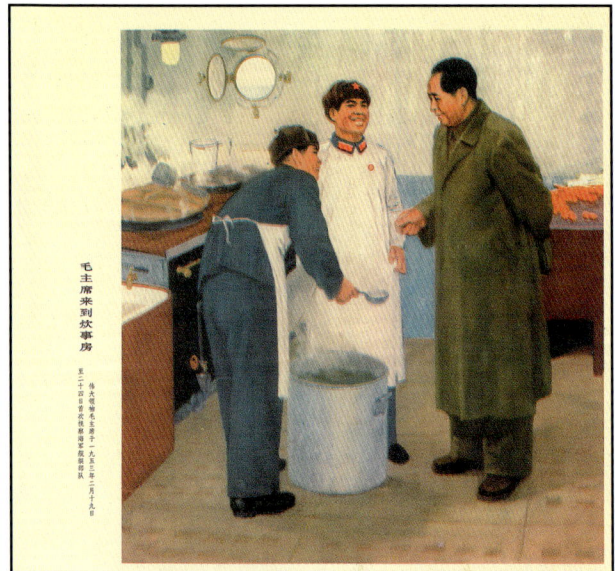

毛主席来到炊事房

Chairman Mao visiting a ship's mess. Print on paper.

毛主席来到造船厂

Chairman Mao visiting a shipyard. Print on paper.

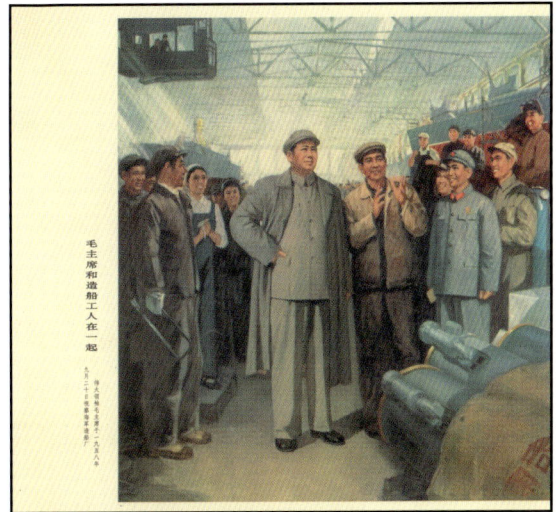

毛主席和造船工人在一起

Chairman Mao with shipyard workers. Print on paper.

毛主席挥手我前进

伟大领袖毛主席于一九五八年九月二十日视察海军鱼雷快艇部队

Chairman Mao leading us forward. Print on paper.

向毛主席和林副主席汇报

亲切接见无海军舰艇部队作战有功的副政委

Report to Chairman Mao and Vice-Chairman Lin. Print on paper.

光荣归于毛主席

伟大领袖毛主席审阅"八·六"海战捷报总报告

Glory belongs to Chairman Mao. Print on paper.

最高的荣誉

亲切接见海军航空兵作战有功人员

伟大领袖毛主席和他的亲密战友林彪副主席

Highest honor. Print on paper. 7" x 8".

最 幸 福 的 时 刻

伟大领袖毛主席和他的亲密战友林彪副主席于一九六七年十二月
三日，亲切接见海军首次学习毛主席著作积极分子代表大会全体代表

The happiest Moment – Chairman Mao and Vice-Chairman Lin. Print on paper.

要永远沿着毛主席指引的航向前进

林彪副主席于一九五〇年一月视察"长沙"军舰

Must forever follow the direction of Chairman Mao to move
forward – Vice-Chairman Lin Biao. Print on paper.

团结紧张   严肃活泼

亲 切 的 关 怀

林彪副主席于一九五七年三月三十日视察海军技术勤务部队

Warm care. Print on paper.

加强海防 保卫祖国
林彪副主席于一九五八年十二月三十一日视察海军岸炮部队并题词

Improve naval defense, protect our country. Print on paper.

发扬我军优良传统
林彪副主席于一九六一年二月视察海军南海舰队领导机关

Promote our army's good tradition. Print on paper.

作风是无形的力量
林彪副主席于一九六〇年五月三十日视察海军院校和岸炮部队并题词

Moral behavior is the invisible strength. Print on paper.

The Capital Club, a popular restaurant in Beijing frequented by expatriates serves a cocktail drink called "the crash," a not-so-subtle reference to Lin Biao's suspicious death.

把无产阶级文化大革命进行到底

林彪副主席在无产阶级文化大革命的重要时刻，于一九六六年九月二十三日视察海军领导机关

Continue the Great Proletarian Cultural Revolution to the end. Print on paper.

伟大的真理

Great Truth. Print on paper.

巨大的鼓舞

林彪副主席于一九七〇年二月二日亲自指挥海军航空兵击落入侵我国领空的美帝无人驾驶高空侦察飞机

Great Encouragement. Print on paper.

Chapter 4
The Red Guards

The sixteen point decision of the Eleventh Plenum consisted of a plan to establish popularly elected Cultural Revolution Committees (CRCs) in grass roots units, from factories and communes to universities and government agencies. This approach lasted only a few weeks, however. The problem with the CRCs for Mao was that he could not directly control them. Therefore, Mao felt it necessary to encourage and support the Red Guards as an alternate source of power. Under Mao's direction, Jiang Qing met with Red Guards and told them things were going to change, and inspired them to implement Mao's exhortation to "Bombard the Headquarters." With Red Guards returning to their organizations and implementing these ideas, all Mao had to do was wait. Red Guards became popular, and virtually everyone wanted to wear the Red Guards' armband. Not only did students want to join, but also peasants, workers, soldiers, and other groups. The red arm bands, Red Books, and Mao buttons became fashionable.

To understand the Red Guards' role in the Cultural Revolution, one must understand why Mao chose students to represent his ideas. Mao recognized the power of the Red Guards when the radical university students posted the original big character poster. The Cultural Revolution Group led by Madam Mao began to identify high-ranking officials for attack, and provided friendly Red Guards with information to be used as the basis for their criticism. Madam Mao conducted private meetings with Red Guards. She knew that in order to reach a broader audience without going through the central government, the best strategy was to use intermediaries with a wide following, such as the Red Guards.

Although wider participation strengthened the Red Guards, it also introduced tensions that would mean their eventual demise. The first Red Guards were the children of Party cadres at the central level and were organized in August and September 1966. These youngsters considered themselves revolutionary by birth and excluded all others. Only later, children with good class background, such as families of workers, farmers, and soldiers (gongnongbing) formed their competing (zaofan, or rebel) organizations. These Red Guards were encouraged to target local sources of authority, such as school principals, local party leaders, and intellectuals, and criticize them through struggle meetings. These struggle meetings gradually became more violent; beatings and maltreatment thrived in this climate. "Monsters" and "demons" were common epithets used to attack targeted groups.

Although the initial targets had been local non-political organizations such as schools, soon Red Guards were marching out of the schools to attack the "four olds:" old ideas, old culture, old customs, and old habits. The Red Guards drew international attention as their actions grew more brazen and dramatic, and they began to feud among themselves. In August, Red Guards and others began to travel around the country free of charge in a program called "Chuan Lian" or "Exchange revolutionary experiences and connect with one another." Their first mass rally was held in Tiananmen Square in August 1966, where Mao accepted a Red Guard armband to demonstrate this support for their activities.

Mao Zedong and the Red Guards. Red Guards in their respective uniforms with armbands, waving Red Books, and carrying "serve the people" shoulder bags. Mao reviewed the young Red Guards in Tiananmen Square several times during the Cultural Revolution. In total, 8 million students came to the rallies. Mao encouraged Red Guards to travel all over the country (**Chuan Lian**) to establish Revolutionary Committees and overturn the local governments, and later forced them to go to the countryside and learn from the peasants. Ceramic statue. c.1968. 12"x 8.5"x 17". $200 - $400

Male Red Guard holding Red Book. Ceramic statue. 3" x 3" x 12". $40 - $60

Two Red Guards. One male and one female Red Guard holding a banner that reads "Struggle against selfishness and criticize revisionism." The slogan refers to a campaign developed during the Cultural Revolution that encouraged people to be selfless and do everything for the good of people, the country, and the Communist Party. Revisionism in a wider context referred to the Soviet Union after the Sino-Soviet split in the late 1950s. In this case, however, the campaign is thought to have targeted Liu Shaoqi, former Chairman of the Chinese Communist Party. Ceramic statue. 6" x 3" x 12". $80 - $120

Female farmer A female farmer holding a bucket and a brush, about to post a Big Character Poster. Ceramic statue. c.1968 3" x 4" x 9". $40 - $60

Red Guard with Red Book and calligraphy brush. Calligraphy brush used for writing big character wall poster. Ceramic statue. 3" x 2.5" x 10". $40 - $60

Female Red Guard holding a bullhorn and waving Red Book. Ceramic statue. 4" x 3" x 12". $40 - $60

Female Red Guard in pigtails with bullhorn. Ceramic statue. 3" x 3" x 11". $40 - $60

Red Guard in uniform with Mao button. Ceramic statue. 4" x 4" 14". $40 - $60

Female Red Guard with Red Book and PLA cap. Ceramic statue. 3" x 3" x 12". $40 - $60

Young Red Guard brandishing a Red Book. Ceramic statue. 6" x 2.5" x 11". $40 - $60

The Unity of Peasants, Workers, the People's Liberation Army (PLA) and the Red Guards. The three leading proletarian classes, as defined by Mao Zedong, were the poor peasants, the workers, and the People's Liberation Army. Mao referred to the peasants as the masses, the factory workers as their big brothers, and the PLA as their saviors. Millions of Red Guards were sent to the countryside, called "the youth-to-the-countryside program," whereby these youth, called *zhi qing*, or educated youth, were to be re-educated by peasants. Ceramic statue. c.1968. 12" x 5" x 13". $160 - $260

Female Red Guard with a bullhorn. Ceramic statue.
2.5" x 3" x 11.5". $40 - $60

Young Red Guard holding a rolled up Big Character Poster
that reads "Revolutionary Big Criticism," a description
used for major criticism and class struggle sessions.
Ceramic statue. c.1968. 4" x 3" x 10". $40 - $60

Two Red Guards holding Red Books. Ceramic
statue. 5" x 2" x 13". $80 - $120

In all thirteen million Red Guards traveled to Beijing to be reviewed by Mao in 1966. Room and board and train tickets were all free and economic activity throughout the country came to a halt. While they were in Beijing seeing Mao, different groups of Red Guards fought over the proper interpretation of Mao's Red Book and the central government's directions. Struggle sessions and infighting continued.

Two young Red Guards. Sculpture depicts two young Red Guards holding a bucket of poster glue, a rolled up Big Character Poster, and a Red Book. Ceramic statue. c.1968. 6"x 3" x 7". $80 - $140

Miner. An iron miner holding a pen and a book titled "Mao Zedong Selected Works." Industrial and factory workers, such as miners, were considered the leading class of the proletariat during the Cultural Revolution. Ceramic statue. c.1968. 3" x 3" x 8". $40 - $60

Chapter 5
Struggle Sessions and their Targets

Though Mao's intention was to use the mass organization to restore his power at the central government level, the masses saw his mobilization of the Red Guards as an authorization to attack everything that was old or counterrevolutionary. A list of people identified as targets of struggle sessions was published, which included landowners, wealthy peasants, counterrevolutionaries, criminals, rightists, capitalist, traitors, spies, and counterrevolutionary intellectuals, otherwise known as the "stinking" 9th category. These, in short, were the "usual suspects" who were always rounded up when criticism campaigns were started.

A number of ceramic statues were created during this period by reformed technicians who were at one point or another accused of being counterrevolutionary. To show their reformed spirit, they designed a number of colorful ceramic statues to demonstrate their determination to leave their counterrevolutionary past behind.

"Taking Chen Zaidao's dog head to be used for the memorial of martyrs." Chen Zaidao, a senior Wuhan military official who disapproved of Mao's Cultural Revolution direction. Wuhan Steel company. Print on paper. c.1967. 0.06 Yuan. $60 - $80

Not everyone agreed with the actions of the Red Guards under the aegis of the Cultural Revolution. On July 20, 1967, Chen Zaidao, a senior PLA officer in charge of Wuhan arrested two Revolutionary Committee members, Xie Fuzi and Wang Li, close allies of Mao who had been sent to Wuhan. Zhou Enlai flew in to negotiate with Chen Zaidao and convinced him to release them. Once they were released, Chen was arrested. Because the incident was not public knowledge, few people at the time knew the true reason for Chen's arrest. The government branded him a traitor, accusing him of cooperating with the Nationalists while working as an underground Communist Party member in the early stages of the Chinese Civil War. Propaganda materials announced Chen's crimes, including the poster "Down with Chen Zaidao." Chen's name is written in distorted characters, meant to humiliate. This incident convinced Mao that the PLA should not get involved in the internal struggles and intrigues of the Cultural Revolution, because the Army represented a separate source of political power that he could not completely control. Another interpretation of the role of the PLA in the Cultural Revolution is that Mao trusted it as an institution and wanted it kept out of the chaos of campaigns and counter-campaigns. The PLA was explicitly ordered not to interfere, but to "assist the Left" whenever necessary.

In the early years of the Civil War, the Nationalists had imprisoned or killed Communists whenever possible. As a result, Communist party members had to hide their status and often pretended to support the Nationalists in order to allay suspicion. In the early years of the PRC, these charter party members attained high positions in government. During the Cultural Revolution these underground party members often found themselves in difficult circumstances, as the actions they once took to hide their status as Communists later came back to haunt them. My maternal grandfather was recruited by an underground party member while working as an engineer in a factory. After the founding of the People's Republic of China, this underground party member became an official in the government of Hunan Province. He took my grandfather with him, placing him in a government position and allocating to him the former home of a wealthy merchant for living quarters. During the Cultural Revolution, this underground party member was targeted by Red Guards, and the Red Guard marched my maternal grandfather down the street in a dunce cap as one of his followers. To the day he died he did not realize why he was a target of struggle. My mother later learned about the connection with his friend, who had been an underground party member during the 1930s.

Three revolutionaries (Red Guard, PLA soldier and factory worker) holding down a counterrevolutionary intellectual expert. The white board, usually made out of paper, indicates this person is a counterrevolutionary "intellectual expert". Red Book, bullhorn, and big brush for writing on the big character poster were typical tools used during struggle sessions. Ceramic statue. 4" x 6" x 12". $120 - $200

Red Guards and Liu Wencai. Liu Wencai, a villain created during Cultural Revolution, was a vicious landowner accused of abusing poor peasants in the days before the Communist Revolution. Struggle session plays were held to document his alleged crimes. The real Liu Wencai died before 1949 and was said to have helped underground communist members in fighting against the Nationalists and Japanese invaders. Ceramic statue. c.1968. 7" x 4.5" x 10". $70 - $100

Female Red Guard and counterrevolutionary intellectual expert ceramic statue. Dunce cap reads "Down with stinking ninth category," used to refer to intellectuals, on the white board "Counterrevolutionary Intellectual Expert." Ceramic statue. 6" x 4" x 12". $80 - $140

Factory worker with a capitalist roader. Factory worker in overalls holding a Red Book, stepping on a person carrying a board that reads "capitalist roader." Capitalist roader is someone who thinks capitalist thoughts and agrees with capitalist ways. Ceramic statue. 4" x 4" x 10". $70 - $100

Male Red Guard and counterrevolutionary intellectual expert. Male Red Guard in uniform with shorts, holding a Red Book and a rifle. Intellectual wears dunce cap reading "Down with stinking ninth category," and the white board reads "Counterrevolutionary Intellectual Expert." Ceramic statue. 6" x 4" x 12". $80 - $120

Factory worker and a capitalist roader. The factory worker can be identified by his worker's cap. The kneeling man is carrying a white board that reads "capitalist roader." Ceramic statue. 4" x 3" x 10". $70 - $100

Two female Red Guards, one female PLA soldier, and a counter-revolutionary intellectual expert. Mao Zedong once said "Women hold up half sky;" women heroines and active women Red Guards blossomed during the Cultural Revolution. Women were expected to behave the same way as men. Women preferred to be described as female youth and not women to signify their position in society. Ceramic statue. 8.5" x 7.5" x 14". $160 - $260

Male and female Red Guards holding down an intellectual. The dunce cap reads "stinking ninth category," referring to the low class status of an intellectual, and the white board reads "down with counterrevolutionary intellectual expert Yu xx;" "xx" represents the first name, which had been crossed out, as part of the humiliation process. Ceramic statue. 12" x 7.5" x 5". $80 - $160

Factory worker holding down a "traitor and thief" and a "revolutionary traitor." The armband on the Red Guard to the rear indicates he belongs to the factory propaganda team. Figure in front on the left carries a board that reads "strong punishment for the traitor." Figure in front on the right carries a board that reads "strong punishment for the traitor to the revolution." Ceramic statue. 5" x 6" x 12". $120 - $180

The efforts of the government turned outward to a limited extent during this period. Some of the propaganda materials assailed imperialism and capitalism, especially associated with the United States and the Soviet Union.

Red Guard and counterrevolutionary intellectual expert. The board hanging around the woman's neck, typically white and made out of paper, indicates her name is Wu. The struggle session occurred in March '69. The targeting of the intellectual class was a result of Mao's distrust of intellectuals and his suspicion that they lacked absolute loyalty to him and to the Communist party. Ceramic statue. 6" x 4" x 12". $80 - $160

Red Guard holding down a member of the petit bourgeoisie. Red Guard holding a bullhorn and Red Book, carrying a "serve the people" bag. The dunce cap reads "capitalist roader," and the board reads "down with petit bourgeoisie." *Members of the petit bourgeoisie* are typically small business people, the professional middle-class, and better-off farmers. Ceramic statue. 6.5" x 4" x 12". $80 - $160

The execution of a vicious landowner's wife. Ceramic statue. 4" x 4" x 13". $120 - $200

Chapter 6
The Revolutionary Committees

What is not widely known is that the targets of struggle sessions were not limited to the nine identified class enemies. Sometimes Red Guards would take it upon themselves to widen the scope of their struggle, and in some cases targeted the PLA. Not participating in the Cultural Revolution, high-ranking officials from the PLA were the next targets of the Red Guards. On at least one occasion the Red Guards invaded army barracks and seized weapons. Although there had been no formal restriction on the Red Guards *vis à vis* the PLA, the Army was considered a sacred institution and the basis for much of the ruling group's power.

Mao, Zhou Enlai, and Lin Biao were not happy about this turn of events. Mao resented the fact that the elusive goal of unity in the country was being undermined by splinter groups of Red Guards who felt empowered to extend his doctrines as far as they would take them. Zhou worried that the development threatened his control over foreign affairs as China's first and arguably most charismatic premier. For Lin the move against the PLA was a further move against him, for the Army was the source of his power and prestige. In the face of this opposition, radical members of the Cultural Revolution Group were removed and more conservative members were inserted.

Soon after, Jiang Qing made what later appeared to be a self-critical speech at a Red Guard rally in Beijing and admitted that they were not ready to use force. Red Guards were forbidden to seize arms from the PLA and the Army was not to use arms against the mass organizations.

Celebration of the establishment of the Revolutionary Committee. Vehicle is labeled "propaganda vehicle" and covered with the slogan "Warmly celebrate that redness has spread throughout the country." Ceramic statue. 13" x 11" x 14.5". $200 - 400

In order to consolidate power at the center, the Central Committee of the Chinese Communist Party instituted what was known as the "three in one combination" Revolutionary Committees. This organization replaced all existing Revolutionary Committees and ad hoc organizations with a single committee that represented the PLA, mass organizations, and unaffected cadres together. Typically, the combined Revolutionary Committees consisted of "reformed" officials, active members of Mao's Thought Study Groups, people from proletarian family backgrounds, military propaganda teams, and factory-based propaganda teams. They soon replaced the local governments. At the central level, each of the three had to be sponsored and approved by the higher level party leadership. In effect, the leadership of the Revolutionary Committees had to be approved at the Central level by Zhou Enlai and other senior civilian leaders representing the interests of the cadres, the Cultural Revolution Group headed now by Jiang Qing and representing the radicals, and Lin Biao representing the PLA. This change in organization marked an effective end to the Red Guards, as they no longer had independent authority.

On the local level, each Revolutionary Committee member had to be sponsored by a higher-ranking leader. For instance, a Revolutionary Committee at the provincial level required the sponsorship of central government leaders, a municipal Revolutionary Committee required provincial sponsorship, and a school Revolutionary Committee required the school district's sponsorship.

The establishment of the Revolutionary Committees was a major cause of celebration. Budgets were ignored to ensure that lavish gifts were procured for senior Revolutionary Committees, with more modest gifts for other local committees. Gifts were also expected on the anniversary of the founding of the Revolutionary Committee and many other notable dates. Members governed under each Revolutionary Committee were given memorabilia to mark the anniversary date. Ceramic vases, candy jars, penholders, etc., bear testimony to the event.

The establishment of the Revolutionary Committees also reflected Mao's dissatisfaction with the infighting among the Red Guards. Once established as a political force that took control from local authorities, individual Red Guards began to turn on each other as they vied for greater authority. This process undermined the status of Red Guards, as it became less clear which of them was ideologically correct, and therefore whether their attacks on other authorities were justified.

祝红安县革命委员会成立两周年
1967.5.5–1969.5.5

你们要关心国家大事，要把无产阶级文化大革命进行到底！

湖北红安县革命委员会赠

You must care about the large matters of the country and continue the Cultural Revolution to the end – Mao Zedong. 2nd Year Anniversary Celebration of the Revolutionary Committee establishment of Hong'an Town. Gift of the Hong'an Township Revolutionary Committee. Hubei Province, Hong'an Township Revolutionary Committee. May 5, 1969. Print on paper. $60 - $80

The Revolutionary Committee is good. Wood block print on paper. $60 - $80

Worth mentioning here is the addition of the fourth and last member of what would be known as the Gang of Four. Wang Hongwen was a member of the Shanghai Revolutionary Committee, where he first achieved national prominence. A handsome man of 37, he was personable and radical, the perfect combination for a charismatic youth movement. Through Wang Hongwen, Mao thought that he might rekindle the youthful enthusiasm that he had dampened by disbanding the Red Guards. Also, Wang's background as an urban worker made him an attractive candidate; as Mao had said, "the working class leads everything." In May 1973, Wang was introduced to the Politburo along with Hua Guofeng, the Hunan First Secretary who had distinguished himself in the investigation into Lin Biao's death and the events leading up to it.

Gang of Four. From left to right, Wang Hongwen (holding Red Book), Jiang Qing, Yao Wenyuan, Zhang Chunqiao (with glasses). Also referred as the Shanghai Gang, they rose to power during the Cultural Revolution after the disappearance of Lin Biao and his allies in the early 1970s. They opposed Premier Zhou Enlai and campaigned for Jiang Qing as Mao's successor. Following the death of Mao in 1976, they were removed from power, marking the end of the Cultural Revolution. Ceramic statue. 13" x 12" x 5". $150 - $250

Chapter 7
Cult of Mao

Most Chinese and people outside China have the impression that Mao always held the highest authority from the founding of the PRC in 1949 until his death. The truth is more complicated.

To understand the basis of Mao's power and his ultimate climb to an unassailable position at the head of the PRC, one must go back to the very early years, such as the Zunyi conference in 1935. After the formation of the PRC, Mao's had attained prominence as the leader of the Communist victory. Khrushchev's "secret speech" in 1955, however, in which he criticized Stalin and the excesses and abuses under Stalin's rule, chalking it up to a "cult of personality," left Mao with a bad taste in his mouth. The criticisms of Stalin could arguably be applied to him, and since the revolution, the Chinese had looked to the Soviet Union as a model for how to run their country.[3]

After the Sino-Soviet split in 1960, which came some time after Khrushchev's speech and, some believe, partly as a result of it, Mao was criticized for several campaigns that had cost the country dearly for very little gain. The Hundred Flowers Campaign began as a means to allow mild criticism of the CCP and a venting of the inevitable problems of modernization and political adjustment. The Anti Rightist movement arose as a reaction to the criticisms, and tens of thousands of people were termed rightists and jailed or banished. In many cases the very criticisms encouraged and voiced during the Hundred Flowers Campaign served as a basis for prosecution of individual critics. The First Part of the Three Flags campaign (The General Line, The People's Commune, and finally the Great Leap Forward) that, in 1958, encouraged people to increase production while reducing inputs, (Plenty, Fast, Good and Frugal) to reach the socialist road was a flop. Some thought it impossible to produce more with less.[4] The radical modernization program (one of the "Flags") known as the Great Leap Forward, in which peasants all over the country were mobilized to produce steel in their back yards in homemade smelters, was an unmitigated disaster, exchanging useable tools for pig iron and leading to famine as farmers left their fields to become amateur steelworkers. This campaign in particular led to considerable unrest among the party cadres, and did not reflect well on Mao's leadership. The People's Communes (another of the "Flags"), a product of the mass collectivization of agriculture, seemed to make the problem of rural poverty and famine even worse than before.[5] At the party meeting at Lushan (1959), Peng Dehuai criticized Mao's decisions in the previous years that not only failed to produce progress, but also in some cases made things worse. Mao responded by accusing Peng Dehuai of rightist tendencies, and undermining Peng and his followers who shared Peng's view of Mao's failures.

Swimming the Yangzi River. Mao Zedong in a bathrobe surrounded by Red Guards and other young swimmers after his famous swim in the *Chang Jiang* (*Yangzi*) River. This event marked Mao's resurgence onto the political stage and the beginning of his rising power. All his life, Mao would follow his own prescription for health and swim wherever he could. Moreover, Mao's penchant for swimming made swimming a preferred physical activity for many Chinese. In 1956, Mao swam in the Yangzi for the first time. It inspired him to compose the poem *Youyong* (*Swimming*), which turned the dip into a memorable feat. On 16 July 1966, a Crossing-the-Yangzi event was organized in Wuhan to commemorate the event. Mao made an appearance to demonstrate his support and jumped out of his boat to float downstream for over an hour. During his dip, he exchanged jokes with the masses and taught a woman how to swim the backstroke. The event was covered extensively by the Chinese media. It was widely interpreted as a demonstration that Mao, although residing in Shanghai, far removed from the locus of power, was physically fit and able to lead China on its revolutionary course. The statue was created to commemorate this event, using photos of the event as a model. Ceramic statue. 12" x 5" x 14". $300 - $400

The campaign failures came at a particularly inauspicious time, for they combined with a series of natural disasters to bring about mass famine and suffering all over the country. Liu Shaoqi took steps to mitigate the situation, such as reversing some elements of the earlier collectivization of agriculture by allowing individual peasants to grow food on small plots allocated to them and sell the food in farmers' markets. Although Liu's actions resulted in an increase in agricultural production, especially of cash crops, Mao saw this as a reemergence of capitalism and used it as an opportunity to seize the political initiative at the expense of his critics. He criticized Liu Shaoqi for following a capitalist road in privatizing agriculture, deviating from the central mission of transforming China into a socialist country. This criticism would form the background of Mao's Big Character Poster that marked the start of the Cultural Revolution in 1966 – Liu Shaoqi was the commander of the headquarters to be bombarded. With his exhortation to "bombard the headquarters," Mao signaled his reentry onto the political center stage.

Mao emerged at the center of a mass movement to attack the governing organs of the CCP and the cult of Mao gained momentum. Mao's *Quotations* and commemorative porcelain items exchanged between Revolutionary Committees were already in circulation. Mao buttons, Mao pins, multiple editions of his *Quotations*, Mao posters, figurines, plaques, and a plethora of other items emerged.

The depictions of Mao in propaganda posters show a variety of intents. Some were made to demonstrate the people's love for Mao; others were made to showcase Mao's revolutionary thoughts, in an effort to implement the official policy to "Love Mao, Love the Communist Party, Love China." In all cases, Mao was meant to be a god-like figure, and was compared to the red sun, a great helmsman, or the father of the country, for example. Often the posters referred to widely know laudatory comments about Mao: "Sailing the Great Sea requires a helmsman; Revolution requires Mao's thoughts" (Chen Boda), "Chairman Mao is the red sun in our heart," "Chairman Mao is with us forever," and "Long live Chairman Mao."

In addition to being propaganda materials, Mao's image served an additional purpose as a room decoration. Mao posters replaced traditional images that were symbols of longevity, prosperity, and happiness, customarily put up during holidays. Those who failed to put up Mao's images were deemed counterrevolutionary. People who had accidentally broken a ceramic Mao bust, if found, were arrested and prosecuted as counterrevolutionaries. Artists who could depict Mao in idealistic ways were promoted to be members of Revolutionary Committee, artists wrongly portraying Mao by not using the right color as background were put in jail.

"Sailing the seas depends on a great helmsman. Waging revolution requires Mao's theory." Signed by Lin Biao, November 29, 1967. For the purpose of studying and implementing Vice-Chairman Lin Biao's words for the Navy's Outstanding Personnel in the studying of Chairman Mao's work. Published by Navy Political Department, pre-1971. Ink on paper. $60 - $80

Chairman Mao is the red sun in our hearts. Poster showing unity of the world's citizens. Print on paper. 41" by 27". $60 - $80

Chairman Mao leading us forward! Wood block print on paper. $60-$80

Chairman Mao is the red sun in our heart. Wood block print on paper. $60 - $80

A widely publicized scandal arose in connection with a painting produced to illustrate Mao's assertion and popular slogan, that "China is red all over." The artist had painted a Chinese map covered with red to illustrate the slogan. The image was made into a stamp and distributed nationwide. Soon after distribution a problem was discovered – the image omitted Taiwan, which according to government policy was still a part of China. The artist was denounced as counterrevolutionary for the omission; by leaving Taiwan out, the inference could be drawn that it is not part of China, in direct contradiction to official government policy. This correction, however, caused a logical inconsistency. Taiwan was not Communist, and therefore a China that included Taiwan could not be "red all over." As a result of this, the Chinese government quietly dropped the slogan, although it remained popular and people repeated it for many years after.

Closely Follow Chairman Mao and march forward into the big wind and big waves. Wood block print on paper. c.1968. $60 - $80

Follow Chairman Mao's revolutionary road and courageously press ahead. Print on paper. October 10th, 1969. $60 - $80

Happy celebration of the Ninth Plenum and gratefully show respect to Chairman Mao. Poster of paper cuts of Mao Zedong and Youth Movement to the Countryside. Anhui Province People's Art Revolutionary Committee, Workers Propaganda Team, PLA Propaganda Team, April 1969. Mao Zedong Theory Propaganda Revolutionary Committee. Print on paper. $80 - $100

Chairman Mao will be with us forever. Shanghai Mao Zedong Thought Propaganda Team. Distributed by Shanghai Xinhua bookstore. Print on paper. Print run 200,000. October 1968. 0.12 Yuan. $60 - $80

毛主席永远和我们在一起

全国的无产阶级文化大革命形势大好，不是小好。
毛泽东

The Great Proletarian Cultural Revolution's direction is great, not just good. People's Police Protection of Mao Zedong Revolution Rebellion Group. Wood block print on paper. 35" x 24". $60 - $80

军民团結如一人，
试看天下谁能敌。
毛泽东

Mao Zedong with Mao's words "the people and the army are united as one; let's see who wants to be our enemy." Wood block print on paper. $60 - $80

Mao Zedong with the winter plum blossom. Mao Zedong's poem titled "Praise the Plum Flower." Xinjiang World Cultural Revolution Committee Propaganda Department, January 1968. Xinjiang, which literately translates into "New Territory,", is the province in the far northwest of China. The residents of Xinjiang are predominately Central Asian Muslims. Wood block print on paper. $60 - $80

We love Chairman Mao without Limit. Wood block print. c.1968. $60 - $80

Under the revolutionary direction of Chairman Mao, continue the Great Proletarian Revolution until its end. Shanghai People's Fine Art Publishing house, May 1969. Print on paper. 0.10 Yuan. $60 - $80

Long Live to the Chinese Communist Party led by Mao Zedong! Jiangsu Publishing House, April 1969. Print on paper. 0.28 Yuan. $60 - $80

Follow the Proletarian Revolutionary Road. Left banner reads "Long live the success of the dictatorship of the Proletariat", and the right banner reads "Long live the success of People's war." Hunan Revolutionary Committee, October 1, 1968. Print on paper. $60 - $80

Celebration of 15th anniversary of the founding of the Chinese Navy. Mao's words "In order to defend against imperialist invasion, we must establish a strong navy" appear on the left side of the poster. Print on paper. $60 - $80

毛主席去安源

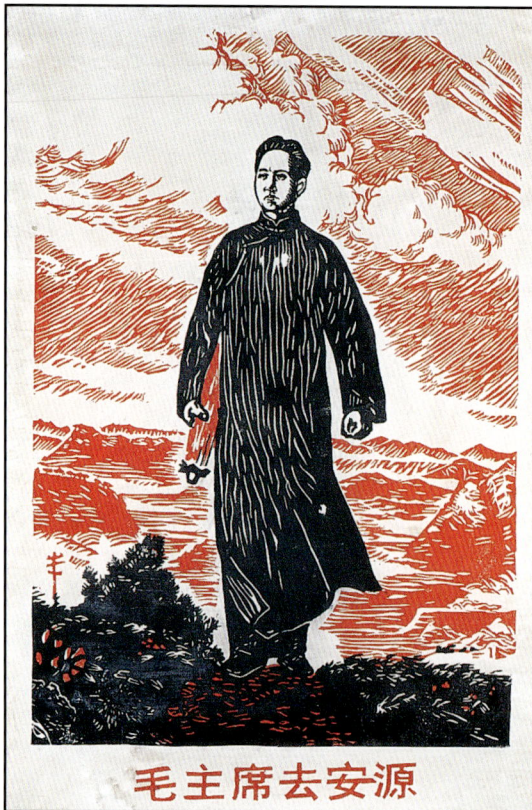

Chairman Mao goes to Anyuan. Created jointly by all the universities in Beijing, led by artist Liu Chunhua, this image is considered one of the finest artworks to come out of the Cultural Revolution. The poster reads "During the fall of 1921, our great leader and teacher Chairman Mao went to Anyuan and ignited the revolutionary flame." Wood block print on paper. $60 - $80

敬祝毛主席万寿无疆

Mao Zedong in a People's Liberation Army Uniform. A poster made from a photo of Mao in PLA uniform holding a cigarette on Tiananmen (Heavenly Gate). Print on paper. c.1968. $60 - $80

Mao Zedong with imprints of "Loyalty" below the image of Mao and "Celebration of Chairman Mao's Longevity" at the bottom. Mao was compared to the morning sun and the people were compared with a sunflower, which turns to face the sun. Wood block print on paper. $60 - $80

赠给上山下乡知识青年家长

心潮

北京市革命委员会

一九七八年二月

Waves of the heart. To "Up to the Mountain, Down to the Village" educated youth (*zhiqing*) from Beijing Cultural Revolution Committee. February 1978. Given to the families of sent-down youth. Print on paper. $60 - $80

The People of China have stood up! The Opening [of China] Ceremony. A depiction of Mao Zedong's announcement in Tiananmen Square of the establishment of the People's Republic of China in 1949. c.1965. Print on paper. $60 - $80

十、中国人民站起来了

开国大典

毛泽东 刘少奇 周恩来 朱德同志在机场

Comrade Mao Zedong, Liu Shaoqi, Zhou Enlai and Zhu De at the airport, welcoming Zhou Enlai home. A photo image of the Senior Communist Officials of China prior to the Cultural Revolution. A rare depiction of Liu and Zhu De with Mao. Liu was later denounced as the "number one capitalist roader" and became the first major target of the Cultural Revolution. Hebei People's Publishing house, 1982 (2nd edition). Print on paper. 0.18 Yuan. $60 - $80

喚起工农千百万 (油画)

陈衍宁、刘案礼、梁照堂、梁器奇作

Wake up millions of workers and farmers. Phrase originates from Mao's poem that encouraged a revolution led by workers and farmers. Yan Ning, Liu Binli, Liang Zhaotang, Liang Qiqi, artists. People's Art Publishing House, May 1977. Print on paper. 0.14 Yuan. $60 - $80

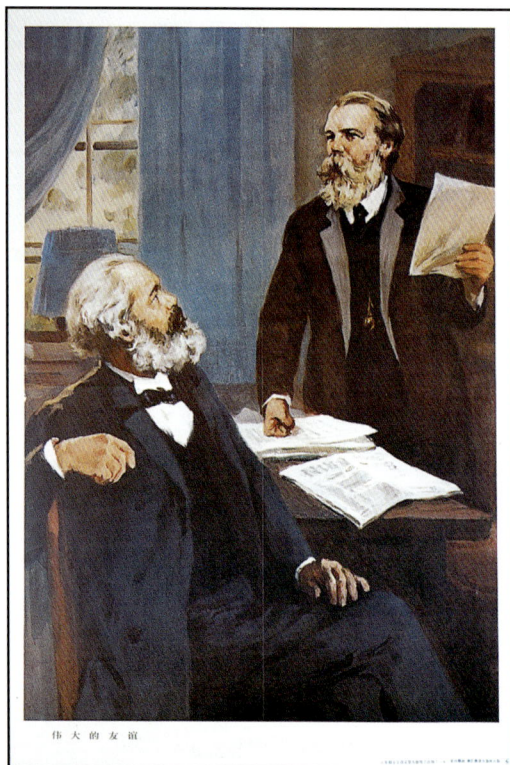

伟大的友谊

Great friendship. Photo of Karl Marx and Fredrick Engels. Sixth grade elementary system 9th booklet (5th grade). Chinese class educational wall hanging poster. Zhangjiang Educational Publishing House. Print on paper. $50 - $70

586-204

One single spark can start a prairie fire. Bottom half of the poster is a painting of a boat and house. The boat is on Nanhu lake in Jiaxing, Zhejiang province. The Communist Party held its first official meeting on the Nahu in secret. The original planned location for the meeting was in one of the foreign concessions in Shanghai, but was interrupted by the imminent arrival of the police. The meeting was resumed in Zhejiang. In the background is the house in Shanghai that served as the location of the initial meetingg in Shanghai. Published by a local Revolutionary Committee. Wood block print on paper. 16" x 22.5". $60 - $80

毛 主 席 去 安 源

一九二一年秋，我们伟大的导师毛主席去安源，亲自点燃了安源的革命烈火。

Mao Zedong travels to Anyuan. The communist party organized a miners strike at Anyuan and created one of the earlier sparks of the communist revolution in China. The leader of this strike was Liu Shaoqi, who died during the Cultural Revolution. Historical documents suggest that Mao did not in fact play a role at Anyuan, because he was not present, though the poster depicts it otherwise. Artist Liu Chunhua, a Red Guard who studied at the Central Academy of Industrial Art. Deemed the most influential poster of the Cultural Revolution, symbolizing Mao leading the people forward. Numerous versions were produced based on the painting. Print on paper. Print run 900 million. $60 - $80

Comrades in arms. Mao Zedong and Yang Kaihui. Yang Kaihui, Mao's first wife, died during a conflict with Nationalist party in 1930s. Poster image became popular as part of the Anti-Gang of Four campaign by reinstating Yang as Mao's "real" wife. Xu Baozhong and Li Zhehao. People's Art Publishing House, July 1977. Print on Paper. 0.14 Yuan. $60 - $80

Difficult days. Long March conducted by the Communist Party in the 1930s, on a retreat from fighting with the Nationalist party. Front images were Zhu De, Mao and Zhou Enlai. Hu Zheyu, artist. People's Art Publishing House, November 1977. Print on paper. 0.14 Yuan. $60 - $80

Mao in anti-Japanese Military University. While in Yanan in the 1930s, the Communist Party established a school to educate and develop party members, headed by Lin Biao and called the "Anti-Japanese Invader University." Liu Wenxi, artist. People's Publishing House, October 1977. Print on paper. 0.14 Yuan. $60 - $80

Mao Zedong meeting with Comrade Bai Qiu'en. Bai Qiu'en is Dr. Norman Bethune, a Canadian revolutionary martyr. He was in China during the Sino-Japanese War. Xu Rongchu, Zhao Dajun, and Yuan Yao'e, artists. People's Art Publishing house, May 1977. Print on paper. 0.05 Yuan. $60 - $80

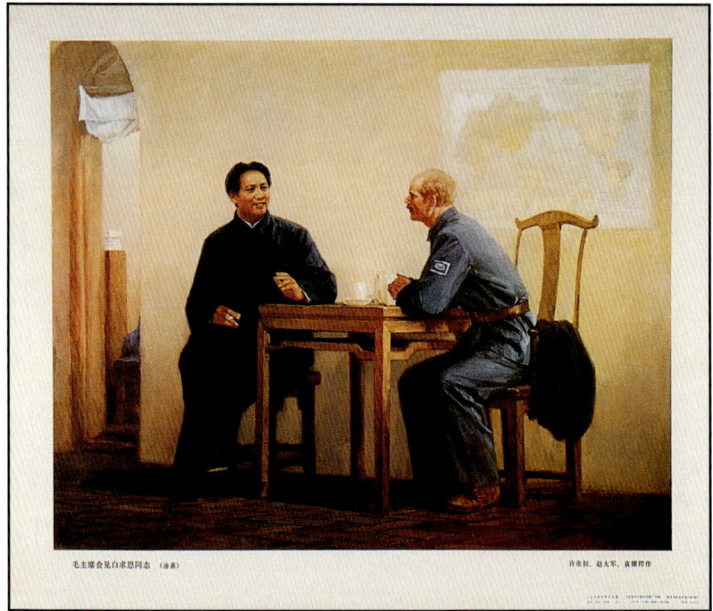

Meeting in Jinggangshan. Jinggangshan, known as the cradle of revolution, where Mao and other communist leaders met and rallied the Red Army soldiers for the fight with the Nationalist army. Li Gang, artist. People's Art publishing house, October 1977. Print on paper. 0.14 Yuan. $60 - $80

Mao Zedong. Wang Shixi, artist. People's Art Publishing House, October 1977. Wood block print on paper. 0.14 Yuan. $60 - $80

Big icy mountain. Refers to a story of an event during the Long March, when the communists were in retreat. In order to avoid the superior Nationalist Party Army, the Red Army soldiers scaled a high mountain near Tibet to reach safety. Many died during the journey. Shanghai elementary school education material. Weng Chenwei, artist. Shanghai education publishing House, c.1975. Print on paper. $60 - $80

Mao Zedong Poem "*Cai Sang Zi.*" Depicts Mao Zedong and his poem, developed as part of the cult of Mao campaign. Liang Gui and Han Xueqian, calligraphers/artists. Print on paper. $60 - $80

Two sided poster of Mao Zedong and the masses studying Mao's theory. "Chairman Mao, Chairman Mao, it was you who ignited and led the unprecedented Great Proletarian Cultural Revolution." Front of the poster - Mao Zedong; back of the poster (not shown) - photos of the masses working and studying Mao's theories. Central Fine Art Academy United Representatives, c.1968. Print on paper. $80 - $120

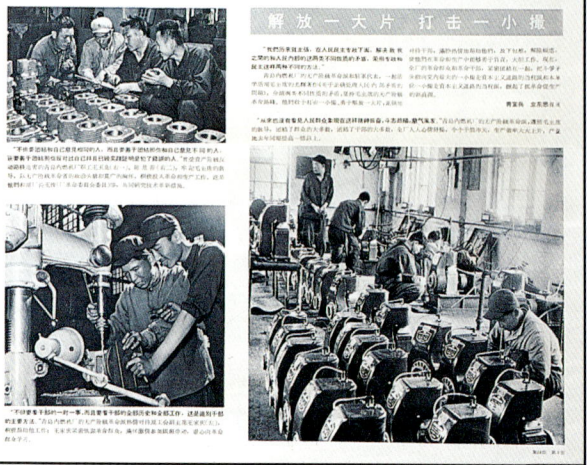

Returning from investigation. Mao visited farmers to investigate their lives and helped them organize resistance during the early days of the communist revolution. Lin Rong, artist. People's Publishing house, May 1977. Print on paper. 0.14 Yuan. $60 - $80

Listen to Mao's words. A group in the countryside gathered to hear Mao after his ascension to the Chairmanship. Zhao Youping, artist. Peoples Art Publishing house, July 1977. Print on paper. 0.14 Yuan. $60 - $80

Chairman Mao and young farmer. Zhang Fulong, artist. People's Publishing House, October 1977. Print on paper. 0.14 Yuan. $60 - $80

Hunan Communist party underground gathering. Depicts Mao with Dong Biwu. Zhou Shuqiao, artist. Beijing People's Printing Company, July 1977. Print on paper. 0.14 Yuan. $60 - $80

中国人民有志气

Chinese People are courageous. Mao Zedong and premier Zhou Enlai sitting with Wang Jinxi, a model worker from the model oil field Daqing, and Chen Yonggui, a model farmer from the model village Dazhai. Yuan Yao, artist. East Shanghai People's Art Publishing House, June 1978. Print on paper. 0.14 Yuan. $60 - $80

远望

Looking afar. Young Mao Zedong and young children. Xiang Qijiu, Jinan Army Political Department Cultural Division. Shanghai People's Fine Art Publishing House, 1978. Print on paper. $60 - $80

Report to Chairman Mao. Sun Guocheng, artist. People's Art Publishing House, May 1977. Print on paper. 0.14 Yuan. $60 - $80

Mao's heart is connected with ours. Qi Wenmei, artist. People's Art Publishing House, July 1977. Print on paper. 0.14 Yuan. $60 - $80

Warmth. Mao surrounded by PLA soldiers. Zhi Ting, Shao Zhenghu, Xiang Ergong, artists. People's Publishing House, May 1977. Print on paper. 0.14 Yuan. $60 - $80

Yanan children's heart belongs to Chairman Mao. Yanan is called the Revolution Base Area from which the Communist victory over China started. Created as a Chinese New Year painting by the Shanxi Art Department. People's Art Publishing House, November 1977. Print on paper. 0.14 Yuan. $60 - $80

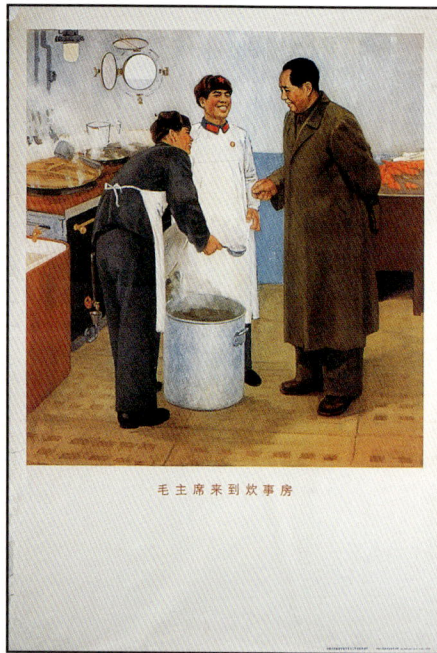

毛主席来到炊事房

Chairman Mao visits a navy mess. In
memory of Mao's visit to a Chinese
Navy ship from Feb 19 to 24, 1953.
c.1977. Print on paper. $60 - $80

万 物 生 长 靠 太 阳

Nature requires the sun. A well
known slogan used to compare
people to nature, with Mao as the
sun. Xie Zhigang and Hu Zhenyu,
artists. People's Publishing House.
Print on paper. 0.14 Yuan. $60 - $80

一九六一年，毛主席在庐山。

毛主席和华国锋同志在一起。

一九五九年，毛主席和亚洲、
非洲、拉丁美洲朋友在一起。

一九五八年，毛主席和新疆维吾尔族老贫农库尔班·吐鲁木亲切握手。

毛主席和朱德同志在一起。

毛主席和董必武同志在一起。

Double sided poster of Mao Zedong with the people. Shows Mao interacting with different classes and minority representatives. Given that one of them shows Hua Guofeng with Mao, these were likely to be propaganda posters used to establish Hua's credentials as Mao's successor. Print on paper. $60 - $80

Climbing Jinggang mountain. Originated from an oil painting. Jinggang mountain was a base for the Red Army in the 1930s. This scene came from a poem Mao wrote to describe his willingness to fight whomever (in this case Lin Biao) stood in his way. Since Jinggang Mountain was a symbol of communist victory, by climbing the mountain again Mao declared a war against Lin Biao. Ma Zhensheng and Zhu Licun, artists. People's Publishing House, May 1977. Print on paper. 0.14 Yuan. $60 - $80

Advertisement for the subscription for Jianghan Study Magazine, a semi monthly magazine for the study of Chairman Mao's Books and theories. Subscription fee 0.10 Yuan. Jianghan publisher. Hubei Printing Company. Print on paper. $60 - $80

Tianjin Heshi District Food Company snack wrapper paper. Include Mao Zedong's words, such as "Revolution promotes production" and "Develop the economy to provide ample supplies." $50 - 80

韶山毛主席旧居

Shaoshan, Chairman Mao's old residence. Tianjin People's Fine Art Publishing House. January 1971. Print on paper using images from the original painting. 0.14 Yuan. $60 - $80

革命纪念地　　革命纪念地

遵义　　延安

Shaoshan and Jinggangshan, hometowns of the revolution. Print on paper. 30" x 21". $60 - $80

革命纪念地　　革命纪念地

韶山　　井冈山

Zunyi and Yanan, hometowns of revolution (4). Huang Zongrui, artist. Tianjin People's Art Publishing House, May 1974. Print on paper. 0.28 Yuan. 30" x 21". $60 - $80

毛主席在天津大学视察。（一九五八年）

作品收藏字號：　6

一九四九年十月一日，毛泽东主席在天安门城楼上庄严宣告："中华人民共和国中央人民政府已于本日成立了。"

作品收藏字號：　6

Wall hanging of Mao Zedong, made in Jingdezhen, with collection number imprints. Flat ceramic panel in wood frame. 15" x 20" (each). $90 - $140

毛主席在天津郊区农村视察。（一九五八年）

作品收藏字號：　8

Statues

In the late 1960s, with the establishment of the Revolutionary Committees, Mao statues were made in the millions to be given to revolution committees as celebratory items. The object of the statues and ceramic ware was Mao, with Lin Biao appearing occasionally at his side.

Mao holding a cigarette. Mao in grayish blue uniform. Ceramic statue. 4.5" x 4.5" x 13". $40 - $70

Mao in dark green army uniform. Mao in PLA great coat, waving. Ceramic statue. 3" x 3" x 10". $40 - $70

Clapping Mao in green uniform, wearing young pioneer red scarf and arm band. Ceramic statue. 3" x 3" x 14". $40 - $70

Mao holding a cigarette. Mao in dark green uniform. Ceramic statue. 4.5" x 4.5" x 13". $40 - $70

Mao in bright green army uniform. Mao in PLA general's coat, waving. Ceramic statue. 3" x 3" x 10". $40 - $70

Mao Zedong in an armchair. Bronze statue. c.1967. 4" x 5" x 10". $80 - $120

Mao in blue uniform, later known as the "Mao uniform." Red ribbon on his chest reads: "Party [Communist] Representative." Ceramic statue. 3" x 3" x 10". $40 - $70

Mao Zedong. Mao in Autumn Harvest Uprising (an insurrection that took place in Hunan Province in 1927. A small army of peasants led by Mao rose to fight the landlords and the nationalist party) attire from 1920s. c.1965. Bronze statue. 4.5" square base x 15" high. $80 - $120

Mao Zedong. Tag worn on left pocket reads "Chairman." Base reads "Comrade Mao Zedong, 1893 – 1976." Bronze statue. c.1976. 3" x 3" x 9". $60 - $90

Mao Zedong in PLA cap. Bronze bust. 5" x 5" x 11". $60 - $90

Mao Zedong. Base reads "Comrade Mao Zedong, 1893 – 1976." c.1976. Bronze bust. 4" x 3" x 6". $60 - $90

Mao Zedong. Base engraving from Mao's poem "Zhong mountain wind and cloud covers the sky, million-strong army going across the river." Written in the 1930s describing the Red Army's Long March. c.1967. Bronze bust. 3" x 6" x 8". $40 - $60

Mao Zedong bronze bust. Engraving reads:
"Founding father leader Mao Zedong." c.1966. 4"
x 2" x 5". $40 - $60

Mao Zedong bronze statue. Base engraving reads
"May the chairman live forever." c.1968. 4" x 4" 15".
$80 - $120

Mao Zedong waving. Bronze statue. c.1968.
2.5" x 2.5" 13.5". $80 - $120

Mao sitting on a sofa chair. Bronze statue. 4" x 4" x 6".
$80 - $120

Mao Zedong. White porcelain statue. 3" x 4" x 12". $40 - $60

White Porcelain Mao statue. 16" x 5" x 28". $100 - $160

Mao Zedong. Base engraving reads "Long live chairman Mao." White porcelain bust. 4" x 5" x 8". $40 - $60

Mao Zedong statue. Base engraved with "Serve the People." Ceramic statue. 6" x 6" x 28". $160 - $260

Mao Zedong. Base reads "Serve the People," with Mao's own handwriting (calligraphy). c.1968. White porcelain statue. 3.3" x 3.4" x 12". $40 - $60

Mao Zedong in early days. Base reads "Chairman travels to Anyuan." It was said that Mao's trip to Anyuan ignited the revolution, a famous image created during the Cultural Revolution. Base was damaged and carefully repaired – breaking an image of Mao could be punished by imprisonment. 6" x 4" x 24". $200 - $300

Ceramic Items

Ceramic Cultural Revolution items were typically cheaply made in one of the few towns where ceramic production was the main industry. Jingdezhen, a city in Jiangxi Province, was known for producing 95% of common ceramic and porcelain ware. These everyday items, such as tea pots, mugs, pen holders, statues, and flower vases, were used for decorative purposes as well as memorabilia.

These days the most common items in flea markets and shops in China are items that depict Mao and Lin. While Lin was Mao's heir apparent, millions of items depicting them together were manufactured, especially by the military. When he fell out of favor and died, these items lost their usefulness, but could not be destroyed because they depicted Mao next to Lin Biao. In many artifacts surviving from that time, Lin's image is scratched out or otherwise defaced. All of the remaining items were therefore placed in storage or left in a corner, out of sight. Now that the Cultural Revolution has drawn renewed interest these items are appearing in markets and stores throughout China.

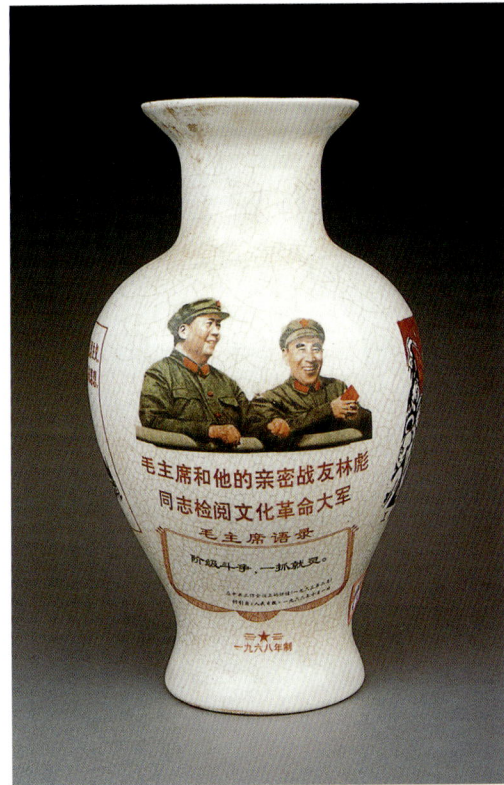

Mao Zedong and Lin Biao, once appointed successor to Mao. Vase includes Mao's thoughts. Ceramic vase. 7" x 7" x 15". $40 - $60

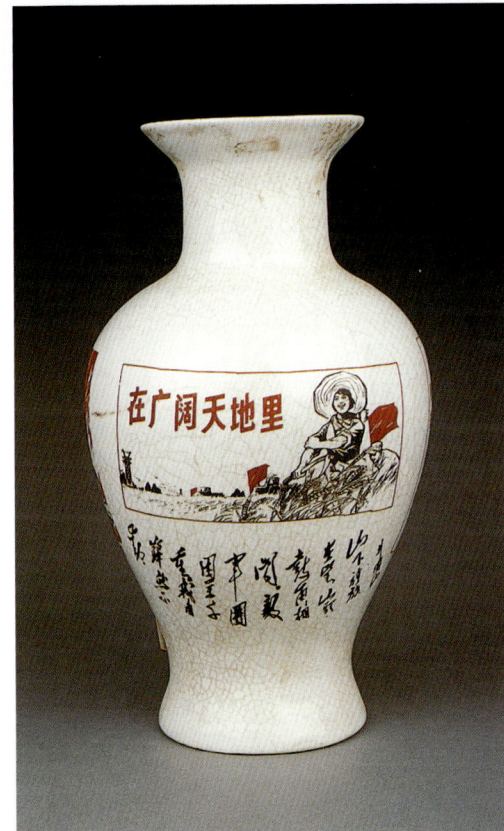

Mao Zedong and Lin Biao. Vase includes bold red characters that read "to greater and wider fields," referring to the massive re-education of urban youth that started in 1968, sending hundreds of thousands young students to the countryside to learn from the peasants. Ceramic vase. 7" x 7" x 15". $40 - $60

Mao Zedong and Lin Biao, with Mao's thoughts written on the vase. The reverse depicts youth being sent to the countryside ("sent down") and reads that they are being sent to the "greater land." Ceramic vase. 4" x 4" x 12". $30 - $60

Ceramic vase. Bold red characters read "unite to achieve greater success." 6" x 4" x 11.5". $40 - $60

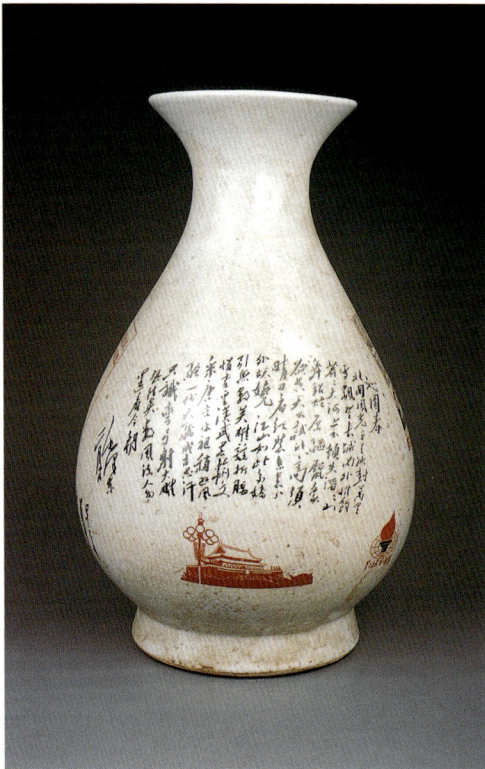

Mao Zedong and Lin Biao. Red building is Tiananmen, the gateway to the Forbidden City. Ceramic vase. 6" x 6" x 15". $60 - $80

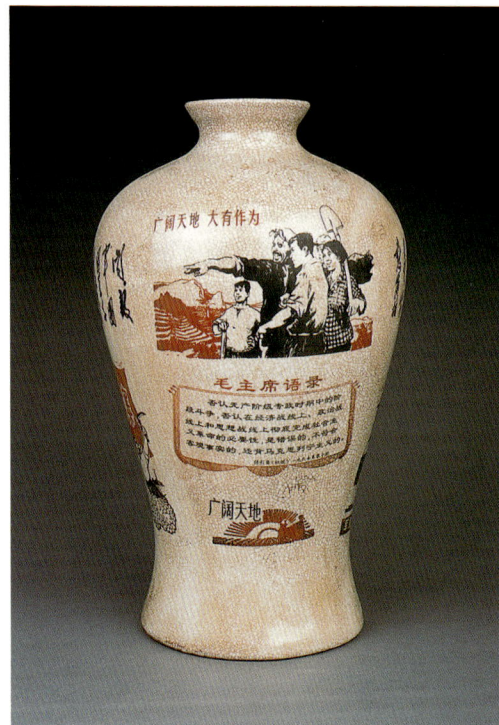

Ceramic vase with imprints of Mao's thoughts. Bold red characters read "to greater fields, one will be making greater accomplishment," referring to the massive re-education of urban youth started in 1968 that sent down hundreds of thousands of young students to the countryside to be educated by the peasants. 5" x 3" x 12". $40 - $60

Ceramic vase with excerpts from Mao's thoughts. Red picture on the vase shows the proletarian class marching ahead. 6" x 6" x 14". $60 - $80

Calligraphy brush holder. Red characters read "Love live the success of the Great Proletarian Cultural Revolution road led by chairman Mao." 8" x 8" x 16". $60 - $80

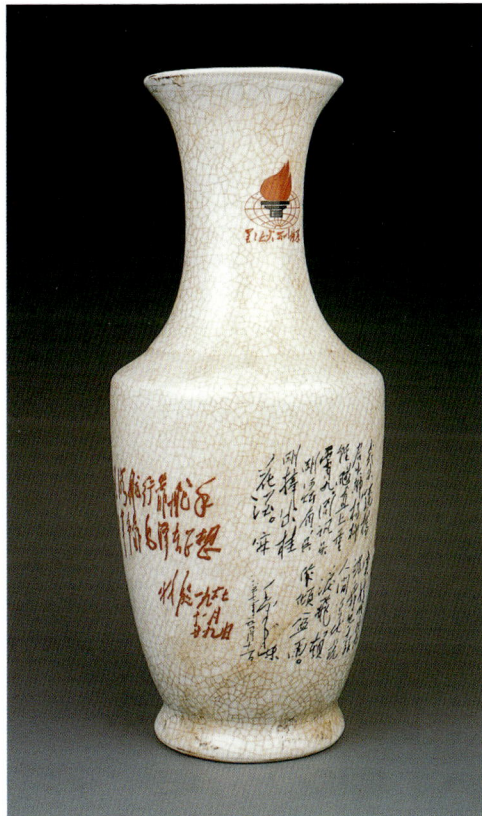

Ceramic vase with Mao's quotations and Lin Biao's words ("sailing the seas depends on a helmsman, waging revolution needs Mao Zedong Thought.") 5" x 5" x 14". $60 - $80

Ceramic vase with imprints of Lin Biao's words, Mao's quotations, the Communist flag, and the People's Congress building. 3.5" base x 14.5". $60 - $80

Ceramic candy Jar. Mao Zedong's quotations written on the outside. 4.3" x 5.12" x 5". $40 - $60

Large ceramic teapot. Mao Zedong's quotations on the outside. 7" x 7" x 10". $60 - $80

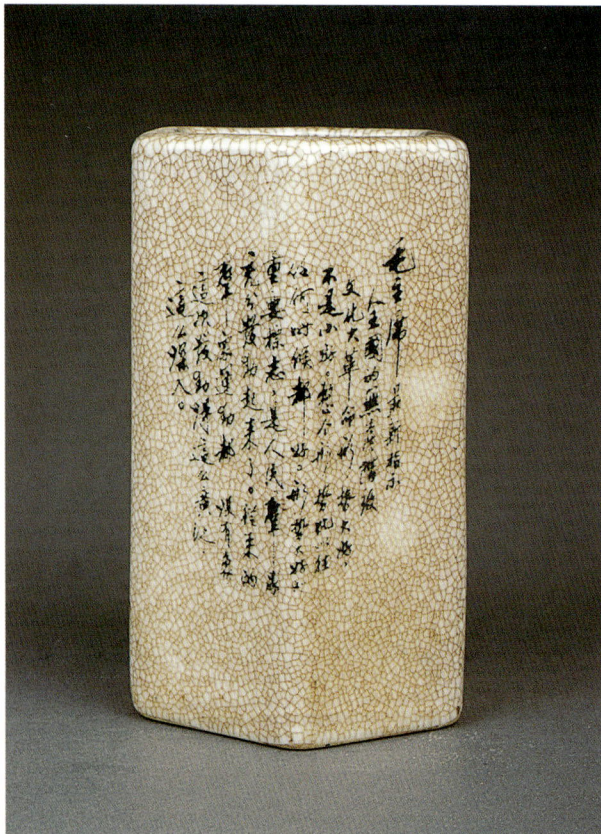

Ceramic hexagonal penholder with imprints of Mao Zedong's quotations. 5.5" x 5.5" x 7". $30 - $50

Small ceramic penholder. Mao Zedong's quotations imprints. 3" x 3" x 6". $20 - $40

Round ceramic penholder. Mao Zedong and Lin Biao. Mao Zedong's quotations appear on the circumference. 5" x 5" x 7". $20 - $40

Ceramic tea mug with lid imprinted with Mao Zedong and Lin Biao, along with Mao's quotations. 6" x 6" x 7". $20 - $40

Ceramic vase imprinted with Mao's quotations, communist flag and Tiananmen. 7" x " 5" x 14". $60 - $80

Ceramic incense burner. Picture of Mao Zedong and Lin Biao, with Mao's quotations. 5" x 5" x 6". $30 - $50

Ceramic Keepsake box. 3" x 3" x 1.5". $20 - $40

Ceramic Mao plaque. Left image shows worker and the quotation of "Industry must learn from Daqing." Right picture shows PLA soldier and the people, with Mao's quotation "People's Liberation Army loves the people, and the people support the PLA." Lower image is Tiananmen Square. 7.3" x 2.2" x 10.7". $40 - $60

Large ceramic plaque. Intended for display on a desk to show one's loyalty to Mao Zedong and the Party. Includes Mao's essay titled "Bombard the Headquarters." Historians consider this essay, and the subsequent big character poster, as one of the key events in the Cultural Revolution. 7.3" x 2.2" x 10.7". $40 - $60

Ceramic Mao plaque. Shows Lin Biao and Mao Zedong on the front and Mao's essay titled "Bombard the Headquarters" and Mao's quotation of "The Country is so beautiful" to promote nationalism. c.1968. 4" x 1.5" x 7". $30 - $50

Mao ceramic plaque. Shows Lin Biao and Mao Zedong on the front and Mao's quotation, "Seriously Study Maxim and Leninism and Mao Zedong Thought, Criticize revisionism." c.1968.. 4.5" x 2" x 7". $30 - $50

Mao ceramic plaque. Plaque shows Mao Zedong and Lin Biao's words "Read Chairman Mao's books, listen to Chairman Mao, follow chairman Mao's orders." The reverse reads "bombard the headquarters." c.1968. 7.3" x 2.5" x 11". $30 - $50

Mao ceramic plaque. Shows the famous image "Chairman Mao travels to Anyuan." Below the picture is Mao's poem, and base reads "Long live chairman Mao." The back of the plaque is another depiction of Mao's journey to Anyuan to lead a coal miner's strike. c.1966. 3" x 1.5" x 4.5".

Mao Zedong and Jiang Jieshi (Chiang Kai-shek) display plate. Image is from the second cooperation agreement between the Nationalists and Communists to fight the Japanese. Ceramic. 11.7" x 2.5". $40 - $60

Mao Zedong and China map display plate. Picture shows the unification of Workers, Peasants and the PLA, the three leading proletarian groups. Map illustrates Mao's slogan: "from top to bottom, the entire country is red all over." Ceramic. 11.7" x 2.5". $40 - $60

Mao Zedong and Mao's words ceramic display plate. Excerpt from Mao thought: "Some say in the socialist revolution we don't know where the capitalist class is, but within the Communist party the capitalist roaders are the ones in charge. The capitalist roaders are still on the road." 8" x 1.5". $40 - $60

Mao Zedong goes to Anyuan ceramic display plate. Famous image from oil painting depicting Mao's journey to Anyuan. Originally created by Liu Chunhua. 11.7" x 2.5". $40 - $60

Mao Zedong ceramic display plate. Slogan reads: "follow chairman Mao's revolutionary road, march forward successfully." 11.7" x 2.5". $40 - $60

Young Mao Zedong and China map ceramic display plate. Mao in Red Army uniform. Picture shows the unification of Worker, Peasant and PLA, the three leading proletarian groups. Map illustrates Mao's slogan: "from top to bottom, the entire country is red all over." 11.7" x 2.5". $40 - $60

Mao Zedong and Lin Biao ceramic display plate. Mao and Lin reviewing the Cultural Revolution Army, with Lin Biao's words praising Mao, "great leader, great teacher, great general, great helmsman, long live chairman Mao." 11" x 2.5". $40 - $60

Display plate with image of young Mao Zedong and Mao's words. To the left and right of the photos are words from Lin Biao praising Mao: "great leader, great teacher, great general, great helmsman." Below the picture are Mao's words. 8" x 1.5". $30 - $50

Young Mao Zedong ceramic display plate. To the left and the right of the photos are words from Lin Biao praising Mao: "great leader, great teacher, great general, great helmsman." Below the picture are Mao's words. 8" x 1.5". $30 - $50

Young Mao Zedong display plate. Young Mao in PLA uniform, "read Mao's book, listen to Mao's words, follow Mao's direction." Ceramic statue. 8" x 1.5". $30 - $50

Ceramic display plate depicting Mao Zedong reviewing the Red Guards, with Mao's quotation and Mao's poem. 8" x 1.5". $40 - $60

Aging Mao Zedong and China map ceramic display plate. Picture shows the unification of Workers, Peasants and the PLA, the three leading proletarian groups. Map illustrates the slogan: "from top to bottom, the entire country is red all over." 11.7" x 2.5". $40 - $60

In addition to the mass-produced ceramic ware, the government commissioned a special class of porcelain items called "Official Kiln Porcelain," made specifically for Zhongnanhai, the residence of senior Communist officials near the Forbidden City and Tiananmen Square. These fine porcelain items were designed by the most talented artisans in China, with the object being refinement and understatement. A common motif was the winter blossoming plum flower, a symbol of purity and strength for its ability to survive and thrive in harsh winters, and was meant to be a reference to Mao.

Fine porcelain ware. Made for Zhongnanhai Huai Ren Tang, the Chinese Communist Party leaders' residential compound adjacent to Tiananmen Square. 1962. $60 - $200

Award Certificates

An item perhaps most familiar to those who lived through the Cultural Revolution is the award certificate, given to those who had studied Mao's thoughts well and set a good example for others. Award certificates were also used in schools to recognize the "Three Goods" in a student, referring to academic achievement, physical fitness, and good moral character. The award certificates were typically awarded by schools, factories and other work units.

Award Certificate for excellence in Mao Zedong Thought. Comrade Dong Jinxi, in 1970, was nominated to be an active member of Mao Zedong theory. Award states that he was able to study it and apply it to everyday life. "Be humble, careful, do not become flippant, strive to achieve greater success." Given by Inner Mongolia Second Mechanical Factory, PLA, Military Committee and Revolutionary Committee. Paper. 15" x 10". $50 - $70

Red Books

Red booklets and notebooks had been used ever since the founding of the PRC. As early as the establishment of Communist Party, people had used notebooks with a red cover to record the thoughts and theories of communism. During the early period of the Cultural Revolution, the small Red Book with Mao's portrait on the cover and printed words by Mao came to be associated with Mao Zedong Thought and carried by all Red Guards. Since then, "Red Book" has come to be understood to mean only Mao's Red Book.

Lin Biao organized the publication of excerpts from Mao's political essays, distributed internally to the PLA. Encouraged by the popularity of the essays, he then published a shortened version of quotations by Chairman Mao, later known as the Red Book. He ordered PLA soldiers to study Mao's thoughts and gradually the Red Books became mandatory reading for the revo-

lutionary vanguard. Red Books with Mao quotations were printed in the millions, some sold in bookstores and others were given to the members of propaganda teams.

Since the Red Book was one of the few things possessed by almost every person in China, it came to serve other functions. Often the books were used to exchange love notes and served as souvenirs for travelers to other cities and provinces. Many Red Books from the period contain cryptic notes between comrades of the opposite sex to study hard and love their country to the utmost, or arranging a place and time to "study" Mao's theories together.

Red Books. selected Red Books from different periods with different styles. $30 - $90

Every Revolutionary Committee and many state-owned enterprises and military units published their own versions of the Red Book. The titles ranged from the very simple *"Chairman's Quotations"* to more elaborate titles such as *"Long Life and Success to Mao Zedong Thought."* In addition, the military often held mandatory classes to study topics such as "Mao's Thoughts" and "Mao's Essays." Although millions of Red Books were printed, they are not as common as might be expected. Often earlier versions were recalled when subsequent events had rendered some of the contents politically incorrect. Most dramatically, the versions featuring Lin Biao were hurriedly recalled and destroyed after Lin Biao's failed coup attempt and subsequent death.

政治工作学习文件

☆

王洪文同志代表中国共产党中央
委员会在中国共产党第十次全国代表
大会上作关于修改党章的报告。

Chinese Communist Party Representatives 10th Summit Meeting Excerpt. Includes unusual photo images of Wang Hongwen, Jiang Qing, Zhang Chunqiao, Yao Wenyuan (Gang of Four), Kang Sheng, Zhou Enlai and other senior cadres. Selected photos shown here consist of Jiang Qing, Zhang Chunqiao, and Wang Hongwen, respectively. People's Publishing House, September 1973. 0.38 Yuan. $50 - $80

张春桥、江青同志在大会主席台上。

Over time, the Red Books evolved to serve other functions. Red Books were often distributed at party functions with blank pages to record personal notes or used to capture a major political meeting conducted at the central level by recording its minutes. An excellent example is titled *Chinese Communist Party Representatives 19th Summit Meeting Excerpt.* It contains the written minutes from the meeting, as well as rare photos of the Gang of Four.

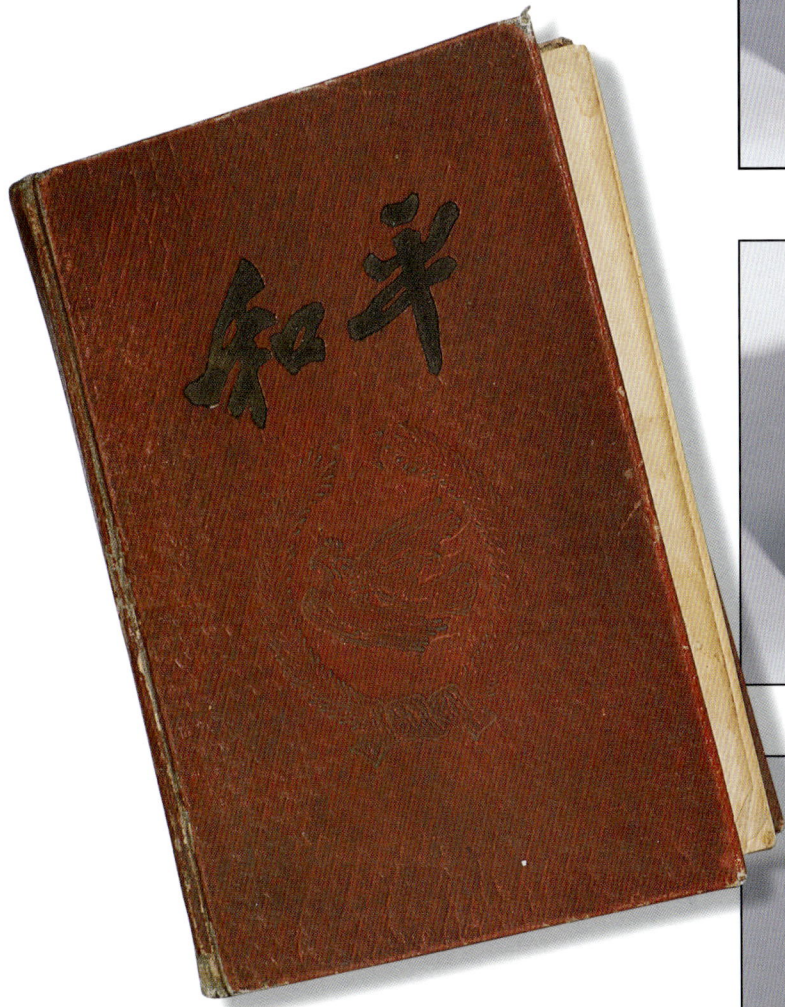

Personal peace notebook. Notes taken by a communist party member on Communist thoughts and CCP directions. Includes the slogan of "Keeping Peace is a task for all human beings" in traditional Chinese writing. Distributed by a state-owned retail company in Beijing. c. 1952. 5" x 7". $50 - $90

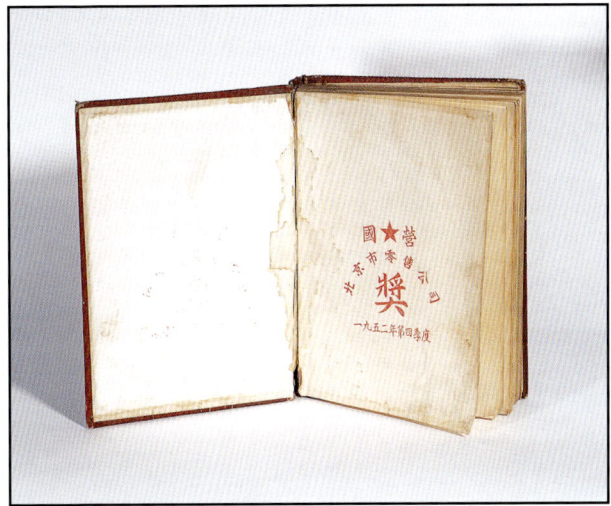

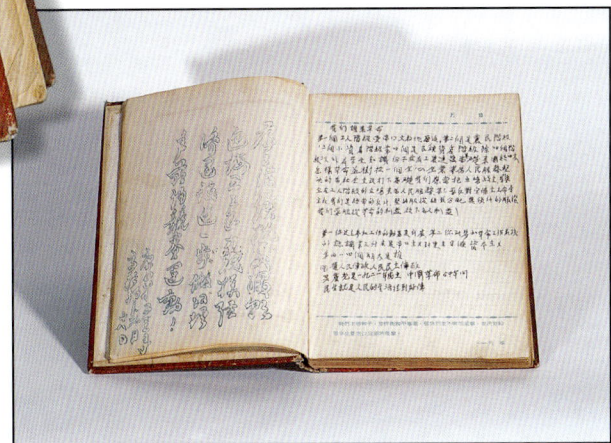

Beijing first women representatives meeting note book. With personal notes on women's rights and Chinese communism. November 1949. 3" x 5". $90 - $120

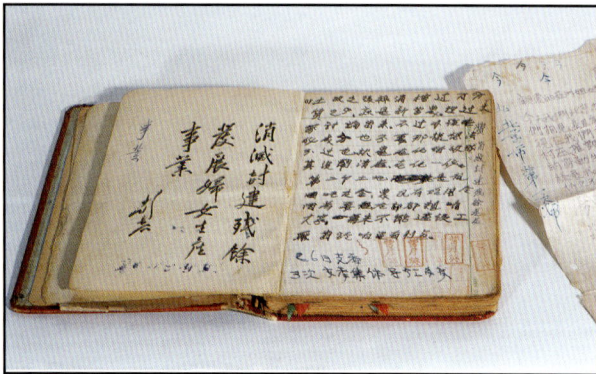

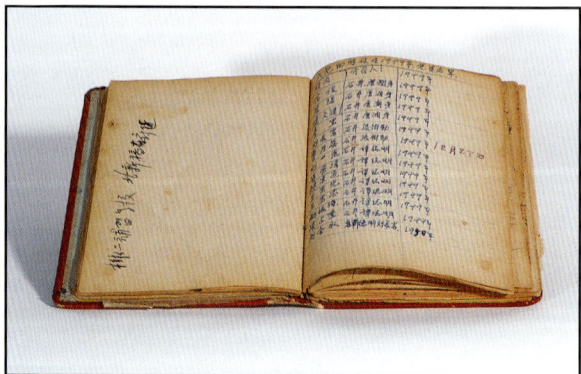

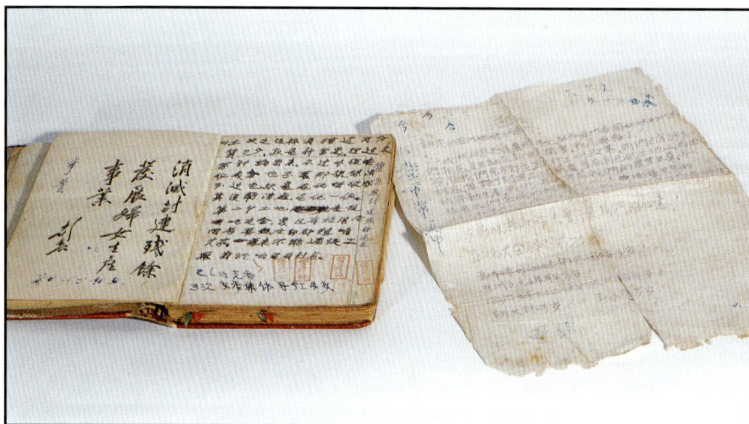

Selected Mao Zedong Theory Essays. Distributed internally for military personnel. People's Publishing house, 1967. $40 - $60

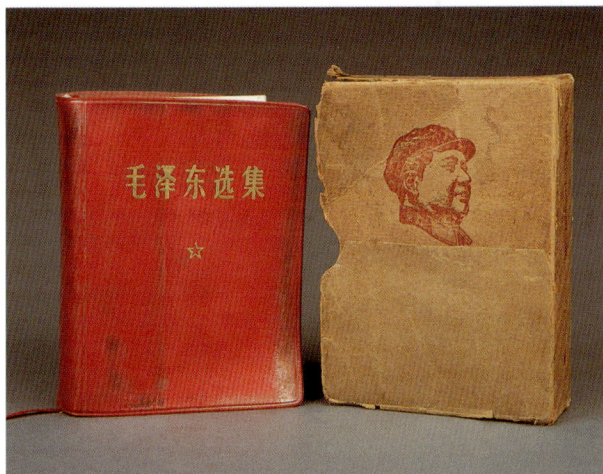

Selected Mao Zedong Theory Essays. Distributed internally for military personnel. People's Publishing house, July 1968 (2nd Ed.). $50 - $70

Quotations of Mao Zedong (Red Book) in English and Chinese. People's Publishing House, 1968. $40 - $60

Selected Mao Zedong Theory Essays. Distributed internally for military personnel. People's Publishing House, Inner Mongolia, June 1969. Owned by Zhao Yumei. 3.00 Yuan. $50 - $70

Selections from Mao Zedong Thought. Cover has the "Great Helmsman" quote by Lin Biao. Essays and excerpts. Published and distributed in December 1968, internally within the PLA. $50 - $70

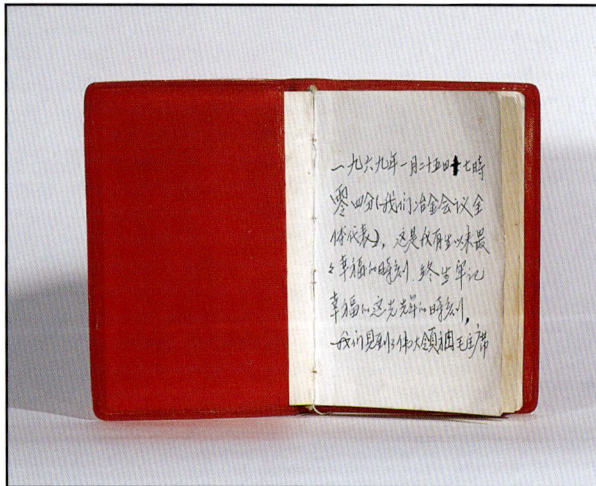

Mao's Red Book. Contains the following, hand written in ink: "at 17:04, January 25, 1969, we (Zhijin Meeting's representatives) met Chairman Mao, this was the happiest moment in my life. I will remember it forever." $50 - $70

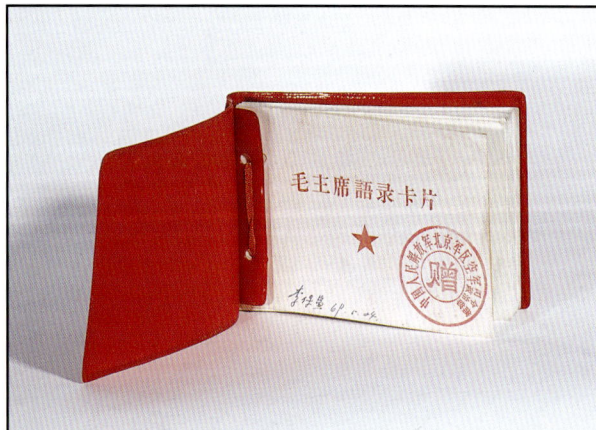

Chairman Mao's Quotations. In red stamp below Mao's photo it reads "Long live Chairman Mao." PLA General Political Department, Beijing, July 1968. 0.40 Yuan. $50 - $70

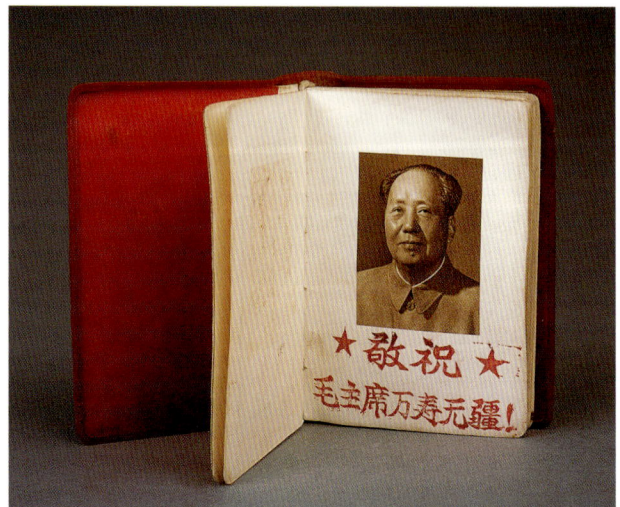

Mao's Thoughts notebook. Used as a notebook to copy Mao Zedong's latest thoughts. Distributed by People's Liberation Army Beijing Army district Air force Political Headquarters. Owned by Li Baoshuan. May 24, 1969. $50 - $70

Highest Commands (Red Book). Edited by Head of Political Department, Chinese People's Liberation Army. Published in Henan province, August 9, 1969. 0.35 Yuan. $50 - $70

Chairman's Quotations. Tianjin Revolutionary Committee, Political Department, October 1968. $50 - $70

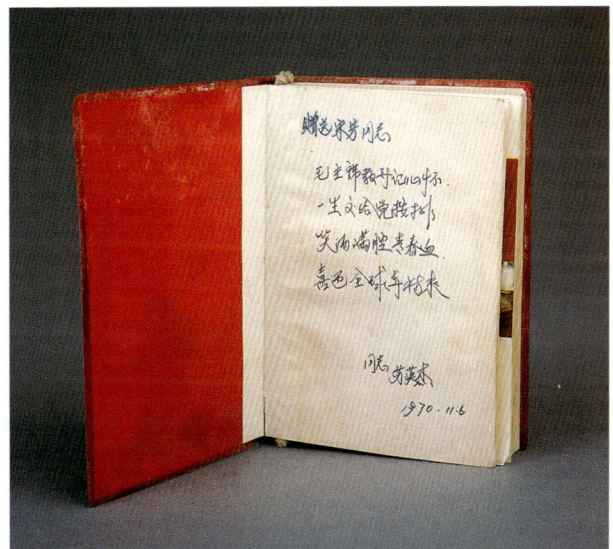

Document of Political Work Study. Red Book, for internal use only. Comrade Song Fong was given this book by a comrade by the name of Su Hanjie on November 6th, 1970. Contains a poem written inside professing Su Hanjie's loyalty to Mao Zedong. In fact this is a subtle way of expressing affection for his lover, Song Fong. Red Books were often used this way. People's Publishing House, August 1970. 0.25 Yuan. $80 - $120

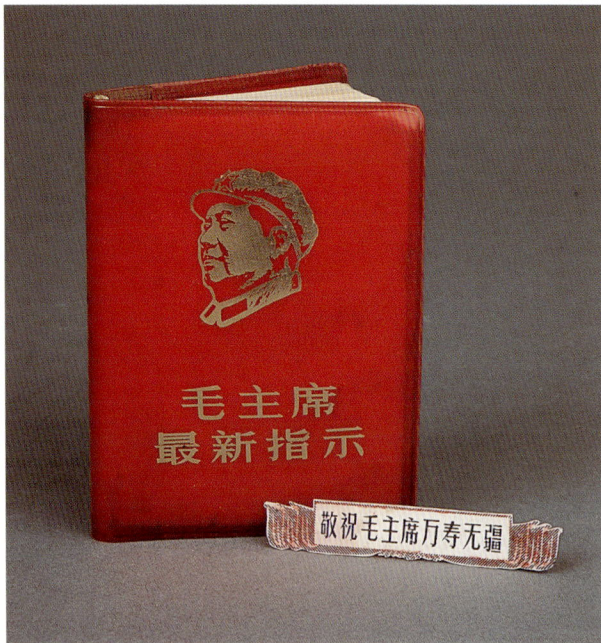

Chairman Mao's Newest Command. Red Book, includes a book mark labeled "long live Chairman Mao." Compiled by Tianjin Revolution Political Propaganda Division, October 1968. $50 - $70

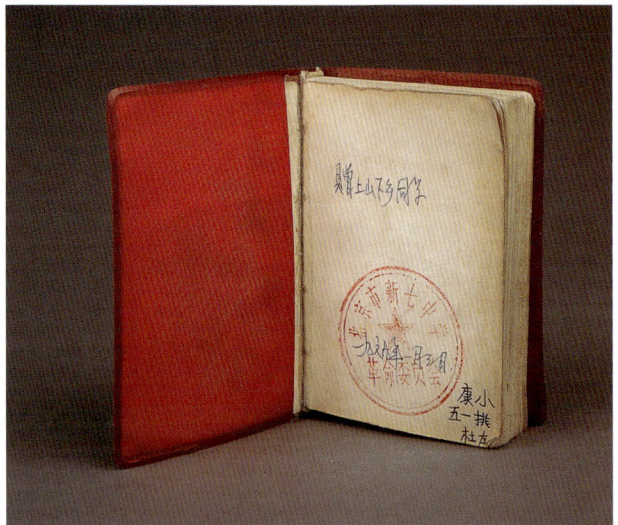

Chairman Mao's Quotations. Red Book with handwriting: "To the Up to Mountain, Down to Village students." Stamp indicated it was distributed by the Beijing No. 7 Middle School Revolutionary Committee, on January 3rd, 1969. Published in Beijing, 1968. $50 - $70

Chairman Mao's Newest Command. Red Book with a stamp that reads "Pay Respect to and Learn from the Red Flag Rubber Company Mao Zedong Propaganda Team," with China Medical Tianjin Li Xin Pharmaceutical Company's Revolutionary Committee stamp. July 1968. $50 - $70

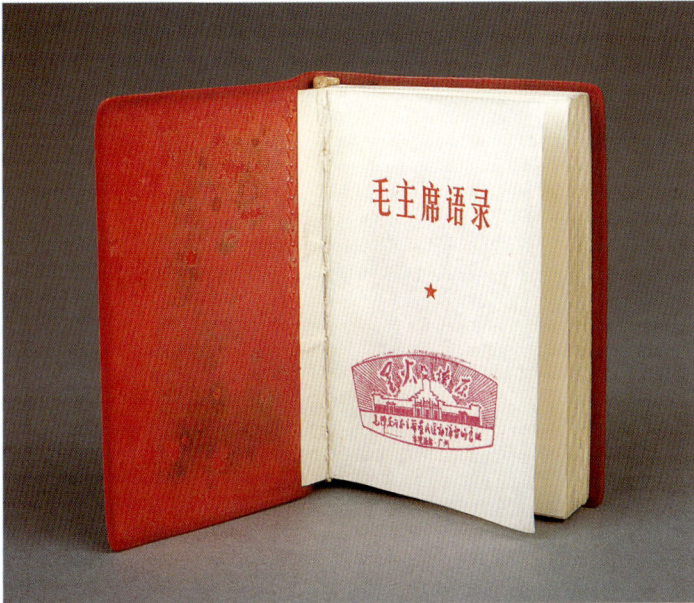

Chairman Mao's Quotations. Red Book with stamp quoting from Mao's poem: "A single spark can start a prairie fire." This refers to the origins of the Communist revolution. The Red Book's original owner purchased it from a revolution historical site in Guangzhou. August 1968. $50 - $70

Mao Zedong's Five Philosophy Essays. Contains an inner stamp and handwriting indicating that the book was given to Lin Yanping, by the Revolutionary Committee of Beijing Xuanwu District, Guang Wai Sand Paper Company, on August 1, 1971. People's Publishing House, November 1970. 0.37 Yuan. $70 - $100

Mao Zedong Poems. A book on the study of Mao's 35 best-known poems, with a number of rare photos, including a photo with Lin Biao taken in Yanan. The book also includes annotations on the words in the poems explaining background on the period when Mao wrote the poem, and further analysis of the poem in the context of the revolution and the poem's meaning. Published by PLA, Navy Division, 1968; and Wuqing township worker's union printing company, Beijing, October 1, 1968. $70 - $100

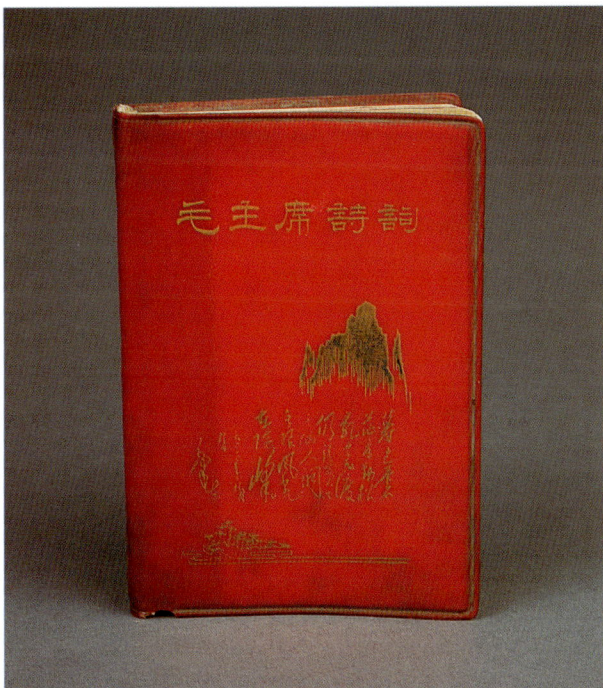

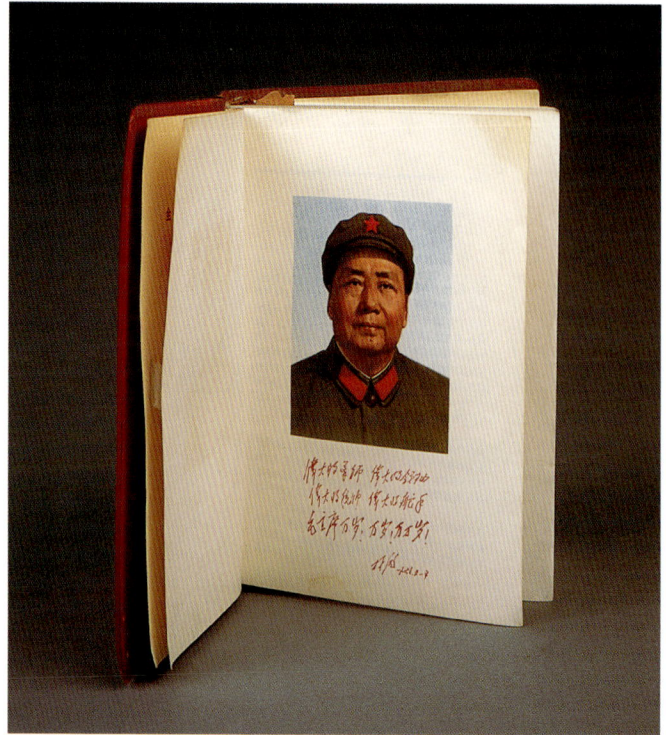

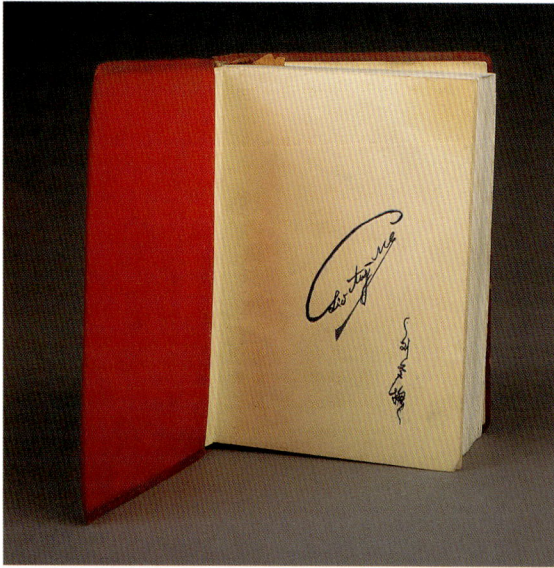

Red Book. Belonged to a Red Guard by the name of Liu Dongmei. Also includes Mao Zedong's photo and Lin Biao's words praising Mao. Red Books containing Lin's words, along with other artifacts of Lin, were mostly returned after his death in September 1971. $60 - $80

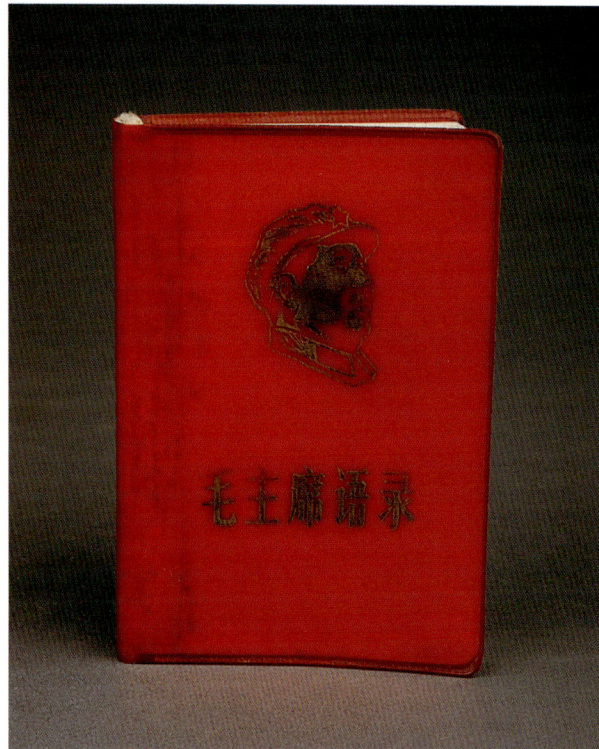

Chairman's Quotations. Red Book created by People's Liberation Army General Political Department. Printed by Beijing Tong Township Printing Company, July 1968. 0.60 Yuan. $60 - $80

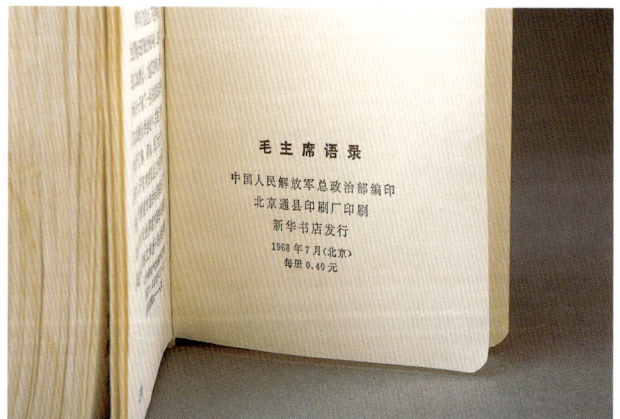

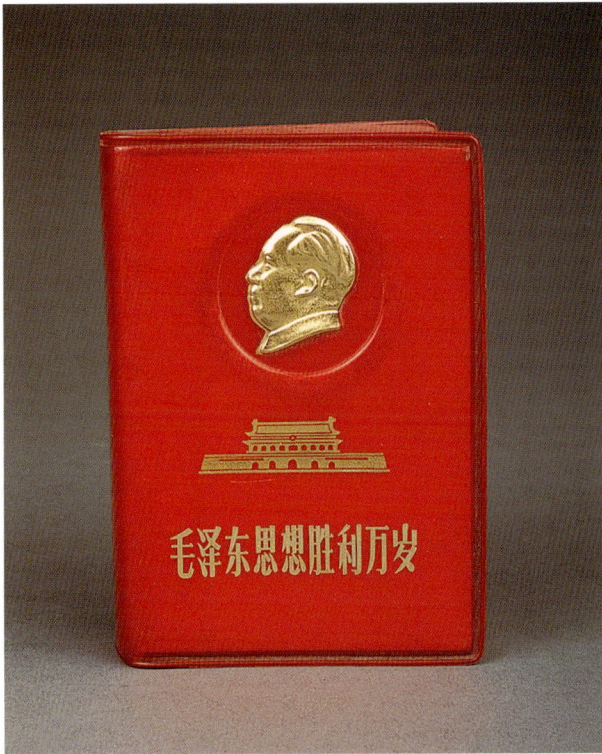

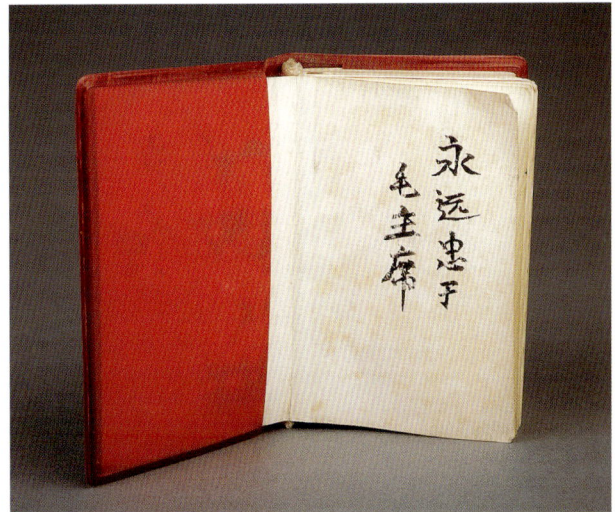

Long Life and Success to Mao Zedong Thought. Red Book with an inscription written by its original owner "Forever be loyal to Chairman Mao." Includes a photo of Mao and Lin's words praising Mao – "great leader, great teacher, great general, and great helmsman." After the September 13 incident, when Lin died attempting to escape from China and was declared a traitor, all Red Books with Lin's words were to be turned in or have his name removed. This particular book escaped that fate. Beijing, May 1968. $60 - $80

Quotations of Chairman Mao. Red Book with Lin Biao's words "Read Chairman Mao's books, listen to Chairman Mao's words, follow Chairman Mao's directions." PLA General Political Department, October 1966. 0.45 Yuan. $70 - $90

The Highest Command. Red Book, with Lin Biao's words "Read Chairman Mao's books, listen to Chairman Mao's words, follow Chairman Mao's direction." Insert shows one of the most famous essays written by Mao Zedong, called "In Memory of Bai Qiu'en, (Dr. Norman Bethune)." The name of Lin Biao has been crossed out. Tianjin Cultural Revolution Printing Company, September 1968. $60 - $80

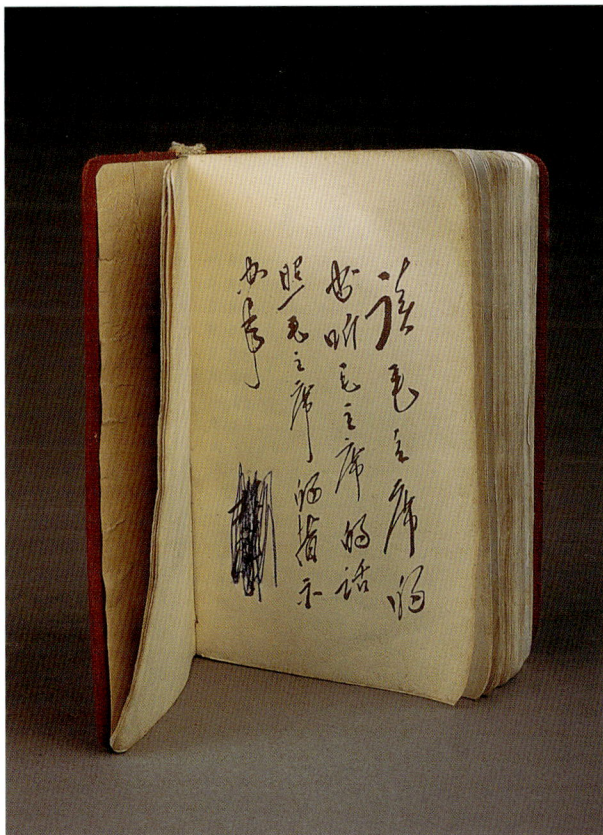

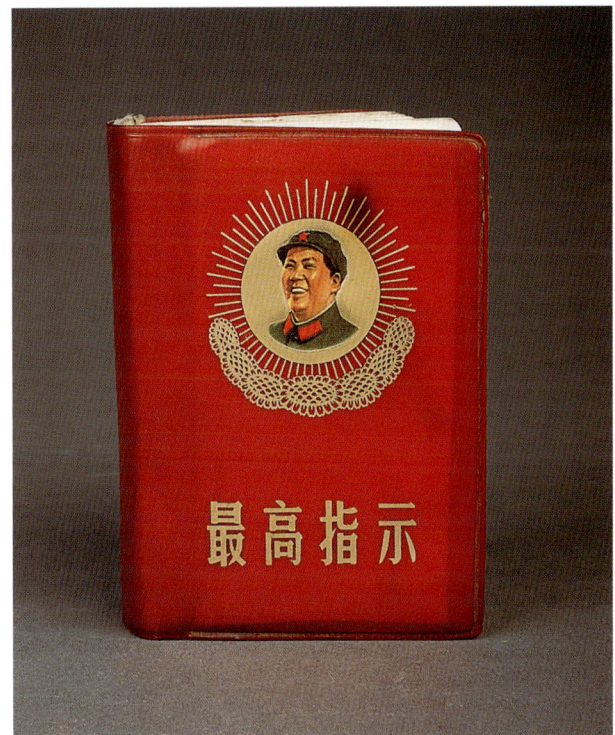

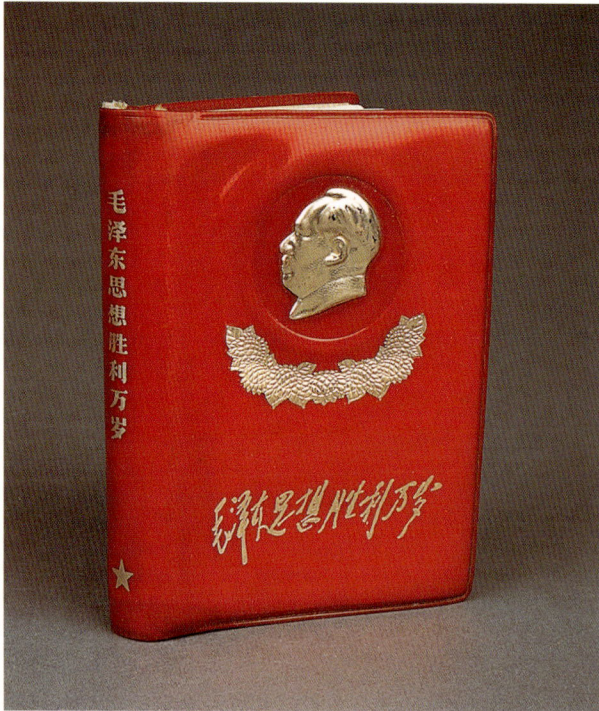

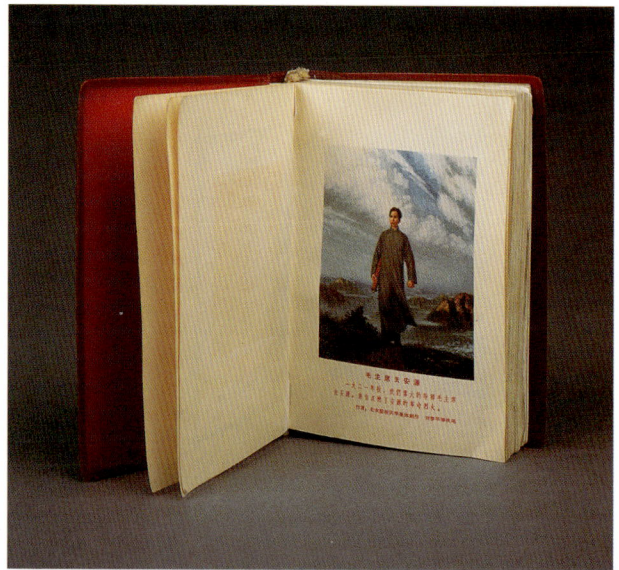

Long life of the success of Mao Zedong Thought. Mao Quotation. Red Book includes a well known image, "Mao Zedong goes to Anyuan." August 1969. $60 - $80

Chairman Mao's important directives since the announcement of the Cultural Revolution. Red Book includes a well known image, "Mao Zedong goes to Anyuan." PLA Defense Science Technology Committee Political Department, July 1968. $60 - $80

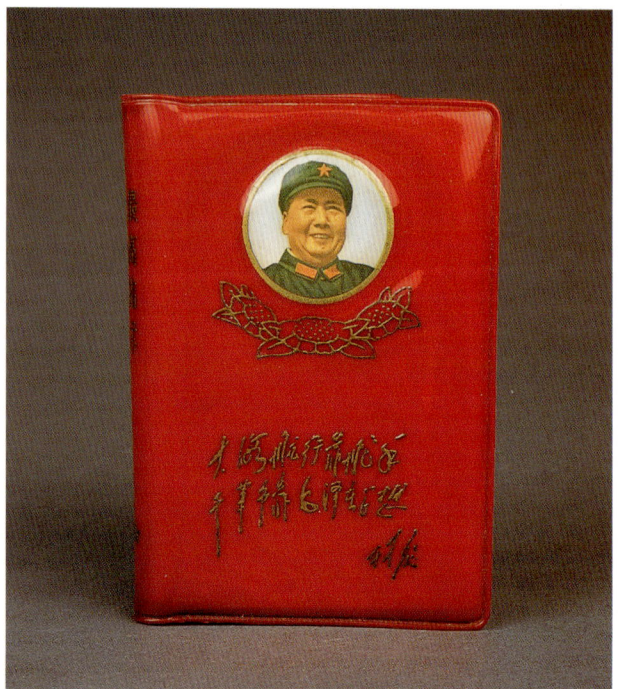

Red Book with Lin Biao's quote: "Sailing the sea depends on a helmsman. Waging revolution needs Mao Zedong Thought." Beijing People's Publishing house, July 1968. $60 - $80

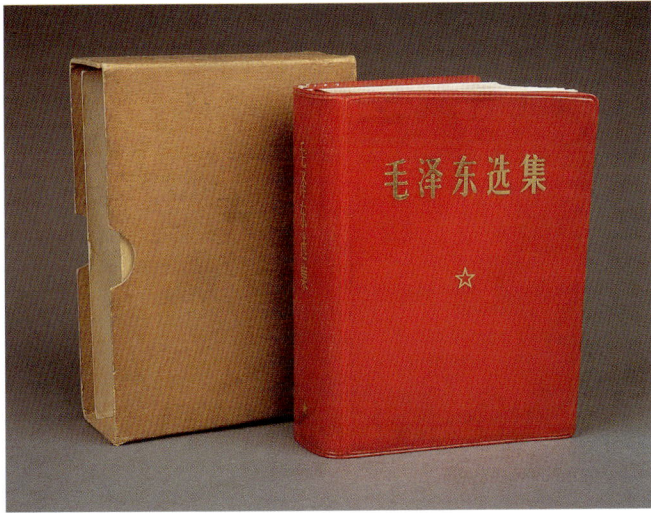

Selected Mao Zedong Thoughts. A stamp on the book reads "People's Liberation Army 3343 Unit Farm." Handwriting indicates it was given to comrade Han Jiansuo, and a quote from Lin Biao: "Sailing the sea depends on a helmsman." People's Publishing House, Shenyang, December 1968. $60 - $80

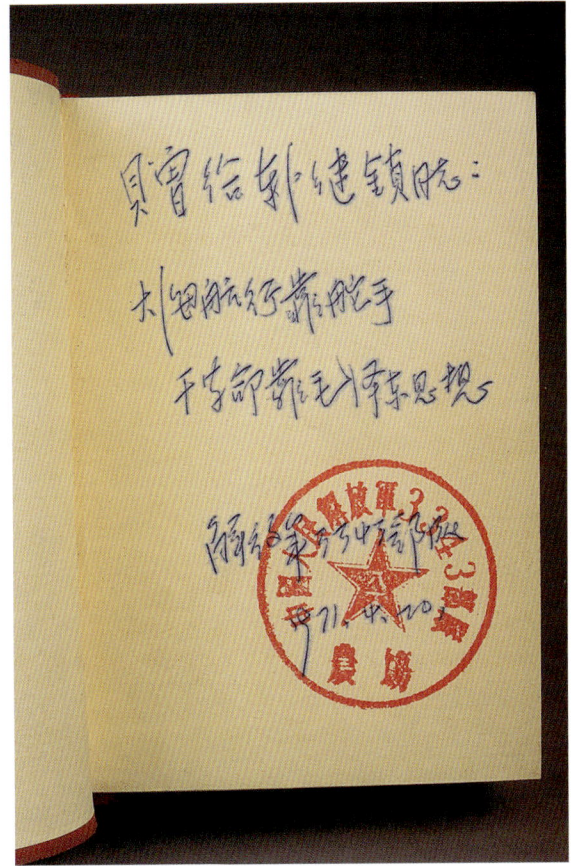

Quotations from Chairman Mao Tse Tung. Red Book in English. Foreign Languages Press Publishing Company, 1968. 0.30 Yuan. $60 - $80

Selected Mao Zedong Thought. Essays and excerpts, published and distributed in December 1968 internally to the Chinese Military. Cover quotes Lin Biao's words on the "Four Greatnesses" of Mao. Lin Biao's name is crossed out. Purchased on September 10, 1974. Chinese PLA Publishing House, 1969. $60 - $80

Highest Commands. Red Book with Lin Biao's words on Mao Zedong. Handwriting inside reads "celebrate the 9th Plenum's success. Great, glorious, long life to the correct Chinese Communist Party." Signed with the original owner's name, Yang Bingchao, and dated April 1, 1969. Tianjin Police Political Department, September 1968. $60 - $80

Mao's Red Book, given to Shijingshan Mao Zedong theory advanced study group representatives. Contains stamp of the Shijingshan Revolution Committee. $60 - $80

Mao's Red Book, given out by Chinese Food Company Beijing Revolutionary Committee on April 11, 1970. $60 - $80

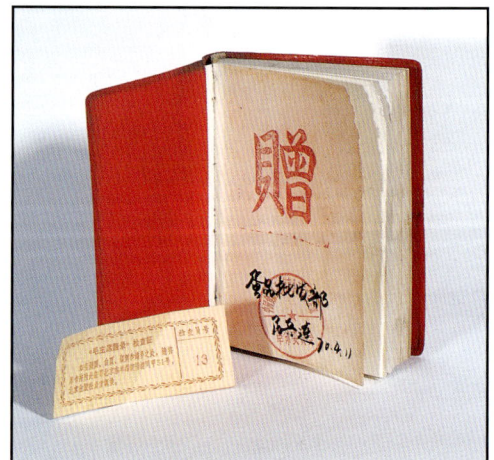

Mao's Red Book. Provided for Liu Hexian, Third Studies of Mao's theory study group active participants. December 15, 1970. $60 - $80

Pins

Cultural Revolution pins were very inexpensive to produce, and the government made huge numbers of them in many versions, distributing them widely. Often produced by Revolutionary Committees, the PLA, and schools, they were made for almost every occasion, from celebration of a Chinese Communist Party meeting to Mao's latest policy directive. Many different types are available today. Often these pins were referred as "Chairman Mao Pins," typically featuring Mao's profile with a red or blue background. The backs of the pins were engraved with a description of the event or the occasion being celebrated. Pins are an excellent item for a beginning collection of Cultural Revolution memorabilia. There are many different kinds widely available, and they remain inexpensive.

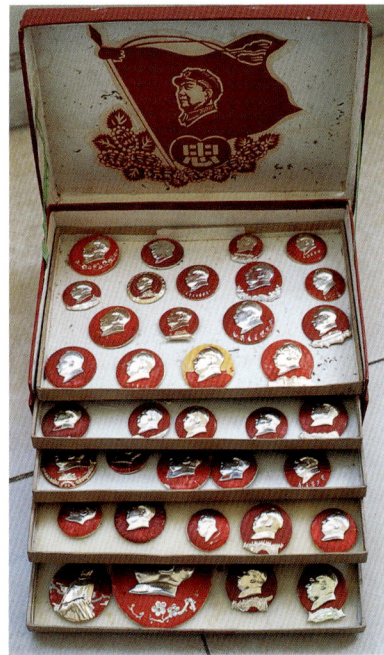

View of multiple buttons. $5 - $30 each

Buttons: Selected pins from the Cultural Revolution intended for Red Guards. $5 - $30 each

Mao Zedong and Lin Biao button. Reverse engraved with "Long Live *BeiDa*" (Beijing University). *BeiDa* is known as the site of the first Big Character Wall Poster. 5" x 3" x 1". $20 - $30

Red Guard Button. Button with Mao's profile. 4" x 4" x 1". $5 - $15

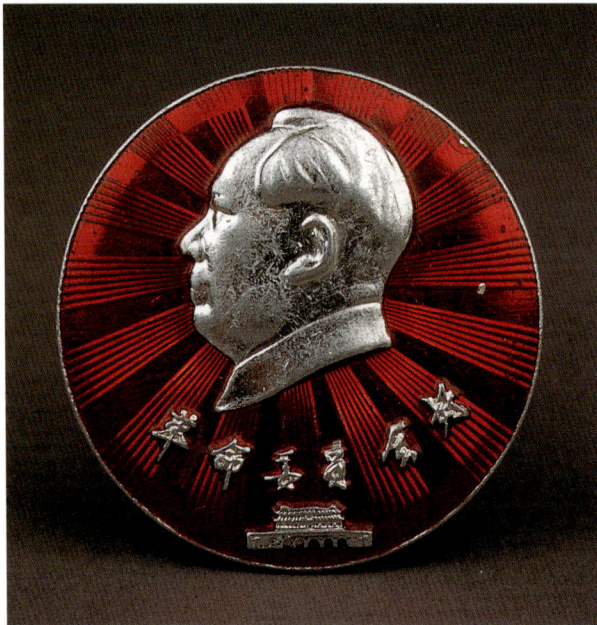

Red Guard Button with image of Mao Zedong. Engraving reads "The Revolutionary Committee is Good." $10 - $20

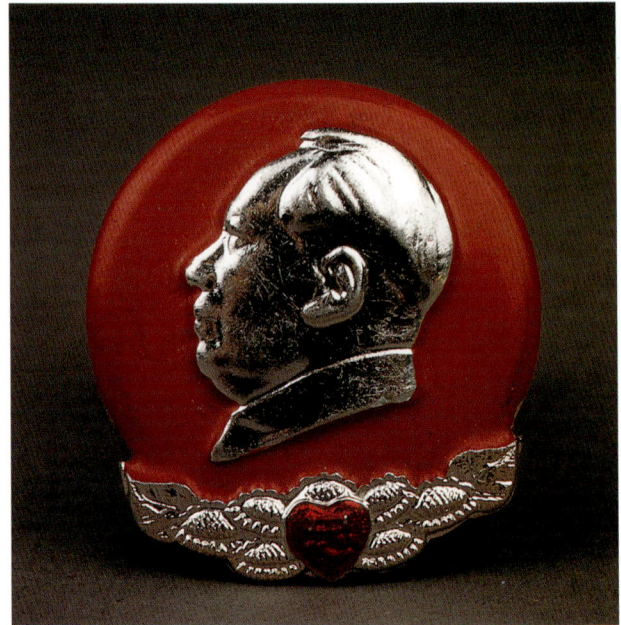

Red Guard Button with profile of Mao Zedong . $5 - $15

Red Guard Button with image of Mao Zedong and Lin Biao at Tiananmen commemorating the opening of CCP 9th Plenum. Made by Nanjing PLA military unit. $5 - $15

Button with profile of Mao. Distributed in celebration of the 19th anniversary of Mao's calligraphy. Reverse has the character "loyalty." $5 - $15

Red Guard Button with profile of Mao Zedong. $5 - $15

Red Guard Button with image of younger Mao Zedong. $5 - $15

813 Army Division Button. Profile of Mao, reads "A precious gift from Chairman Mao to the worker and peasant propaganda teams." August 5th, 1968. $5 - $15

Button with Mao Zedong Theory inscription. Inscription reads "Long live the success of Mao Zedong theory." and "Support Vietnam against the US, serve the people of the world." $15 - $30

Button depicting young Mao. Made and distributed in celebration of Chairman Mao's 75th birthday. $5 - $15

Button with profile of Mao. Produced by 539 Military Headquarters. $5 - $15

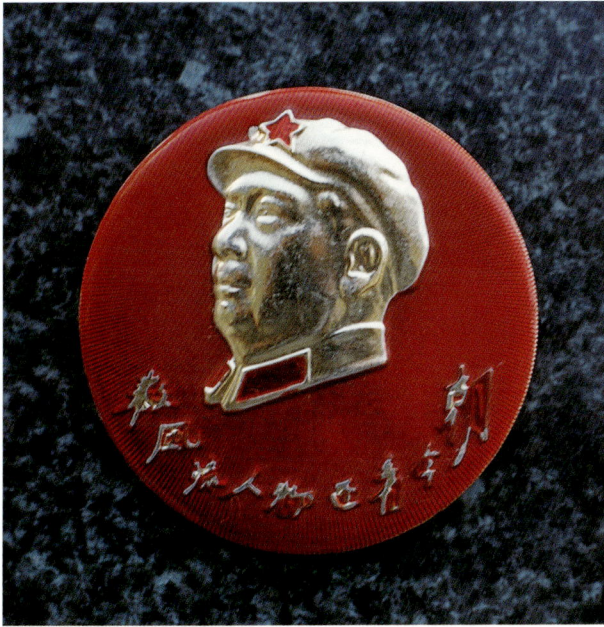

Button with profile of Mao in PLA cap. Below the picture is a poem excerpt: "in looking back at all the glorious people in Chinese history, nobody exceeds the Chinese people of today." Reverse reads "long live Chairman Mao." Produced by MZD theory study group of Guilin City. $15 - $30

Button with profile of Mao. Below the picture is a depiction of Mao's home town, Shaoshan. Produced by 601 Factory Revolutionary Committee for its one-year anniversary. $15 - $30

Button with profile of Mao. Below the profile is a poem, "spring has come, and the plum flower, though very pretty, does not compete with the spring, but simply reports its arrival." $15 - $30

Button with Mao profile. Reverse indicates that the button belonged to Beijing military district athletic team Revolutionary Committee. Made in celebration of 9th plenum, 1968. $15 - $30

Other Items

Other everyday items available during the Cultural Revolution are watches and clocks with Mao or revolutionary themes on the face, shoulder bags with Mao's quote "serve the people," and PLA caps. They were practical, plentiful, and useful for daily life.

Mao watches have become very popular since Mao's Memorial in 1993. Although not widely available during the Cultural Revolution, large numbers were produced for the Mao Memorial and the unsold inventory has been widely distributed. The Chinese currently produce replicas of these watches and they are widely available. Because the watches are manufactured using the same materials and techniques as the originals, it is very difficult to tell whether a particular watch is a current replica or of earlier provenance.[6] One very popular design depicts Mao against a red or blue background, with his arm waving, animated by the watch's movement. This watch has been nicknamed the "Mickey Mao" watch.

Wind-up Mao watches with waving hand. $50 - $80

Mao alarm clocks, round orange and red with bells. c.1970. 4" x 2.5" x 7.5". $40 – $60

Mao alarm clock, fan shape chrome with bells.
c.1970, 6" x 2" x 8". $40 – $60

Mao clock. Minute hand is a fighter plane, a reference to
China's military development. c.1969. 4" x 2.5" x 8". $40 – $60

Mao alarm clock, round chrome with bells. Red flag in background and waving Red Guard hand. c.1969. 6" x 3" x 6". $40 – $60

Mao alarm clock, round chrome with bells. c.1970. 6" x 3" x 6". $40 – $60

Mao alarm clocks, small round, green and blue with bells. c.1970. 5" x 2.5" x 5". $40 – $60

Mao alarm clock, red oval with bells. c.1971. 4.5" x 2.5" x 5".
$40 – $60

Mao alarm clock, light green round with wooden legs and bells.
c.1968. 5" x 2.5" x 7". $40 – $60

Mao alarm clock, small chrome with bells. c.1971. 4" x 2.5" x 5".
$40 – $60

Mao alarm clock, eggshell round with bells. ca.1971. 4" x 2" x 5".
$40 – $60

Red Guard Bag also known as the "Serve the People" bag. These shoulder bags were wildly popular during the Cultural Revolution for carrying Red Books, pens and notebooks. c.1968. Total length 38" with strap. $20 - $40

People's Liberation Amy cap worn by Red Guards as part of their uniform. PLA uniforms were popular as a result of Mao Zedong's "Learn from the PLA" campaign. c.1976. $10 - $20

Chapter 8
The Education of
The Great Proletarian Class

After Lin Biao's demise, the momentum of Cultural Revolution slowed considerably. Those who had thought the Cultural Revolution was going to lead China straight into a new socialist society became discouraged after seeing the previously esteemed Lin Biao branded a criminal and traitor after his suspicious death. There was a noticeable change in the political atmosphere.

In the early 1970s, Mao realized that the mass adoration and focus on him as the center of the Cultural Revolution might actually undermine his power. He even stated openly to "not establish personal worship (of me)." At Mao's direction, the country's propaganda materials demonstrated a noticeable shift from the direct promotion of Mao to "educational" materials. Propaganda materials became more diverse as Chinese citizens were exhorted to learn from the great proletarian class and from revolutionary heroes and martyrs, drawing attention away from Mao. Below are major doctrines the government focused on with its propaganda materials.

Madam Mao (Jiang Qing) holding a Red Book. Jiang married Mao in Yanan in the 1930s and rose to political prominence during the Cultural Revolution. She created the Revolutionary Ballets and Modern Revolutionary Peking Operas with Lin Biao, and was later blamed for the chaos created in Cultural Revolution as part of the Gang of Four. She was sentenced to life imprisonment in 1983, and allegedly committed suicide in 1991. c.1968. Ceramic statue. 14.5" x 3" x 4". $50 - $70

Mao Zedong and Madam Mao. Madam Mao described herself as Mao's best pupil. Ceramic set depicts Mao and Madam Mao having tea while Mao dictates his revolutionary theories. Tea table has a pack of Mao's cigarette, *Zhong Hua* brand, teacup and an ashtray. c.1969-1976. Madam Mao 4" x 5" x 8". Mao 4" x 5" x 8". Tea table 6" x 2" x 4". $200 - $300

Doctrine No. 1 – Never forget class struggle.

After Lin Biao's death, Jiang Qing, also known as Madam Mao, took on a more significant role in the direction of the Cultural Revolution. In the early 1960s, she started revising Peking operas by adding revolutionary themes. By the late 1960s, a number of Peking Operas, Ballets, and Symphonies had been produced. Called Revolution Model Plays (*geming yangbanxi*), these operas and ballets spread throughout China. PLA dance groups performed these plays in local areas and later the propaganda teams in military and work units performed their own versions as part of political education programs. Under her guidance, modern revolutionary Peking operas and ballets took the country by storm. Authors built upon traditional Peking opera themes to tell stories of class struggle, in many cases indirectly referring to contemporary political figures and events.

These plays and ballets, subsequently made into movies, became a major part of mainstream culture during the Cultural Revolution. Virtually everyone watched them, learning the songs by heart and repeating them during political meetings. Children incorporated the revolutionary themes and story lines into their play, much as American children traditionally played out the roles of cops and robbers or cowboys and Indians. Parents dressed their children in costumes from these plays as well.

Follow Chairman Mao's revolutionary art route, successfully march forward. Displays characters from Revolutionary Peking Operas and Ballets. Tianjin People's Art Publishing house, ca.1971. Print on paper. $60 - $80

Propaganda materials, such as posters and statues, were created based on characters and scenes from the plays. A typical gift for a newlywed couple at the time was a color ceramic statue of Da Chun and Xi Er, a revolutionary couple from the Revolution Ballet *The White-Haired Girl,* as a gesture of congratulations to the couple.

Modern Revolution Ballet. *The White-Haired Girl* poster. Originally a play in the tradition of the rice planting song (*yangge*), it was converted into a "revolutionary model play" in 1967, and was selected by Jiang Qing (Madam Mao) for nationwide performance. It is a story about class struggle and triumphs of people over the bitter suppression of class enemies, such as the vicious landowner Huang Shiren who caused the death of the white-haired girl's father. Hebei People's Publishing House, August 1972. Print on paper. 0.14 Yuan. $80 - $100

革命现代舞剧

白毛女

红太阳照亮了杨各庄

The white-haired girl (*Bai Mao Nü*). Scene from the well known revolutionary ballet, or modern revolutionary play, *The White- Haired Girl.* Ceramic statue. 3" x 8" x 13". $40 - $60

The white-haired girl with class enemy, from the revolutionary ballet Bai Mao Nü, *The White-haired Girl*. Depiction of the white haired girl fighting against class enemies – Huang Shiren, abusive landowner, and Mu Renzhi, traitor and Nationalist party sympathizer. Ceramic statue. 8" x 5" x 14". $80 - $100

The white-haired girl with Da Chun, from *The White-Haired Girl*. Da Chun is a main character who joined the Red Army and brought them back to his town to rescue them from suppression by the vicious landowners. Ceramic statue. 7" x 5" x 12". $80 - $100

The People have risen. Scene from *The White-Haired Girl*. Da Chun and the villagers. Ceramic statue. 7" x 4" 11". $160 - $240

Modern revolutionary ballet *White-Haired Girl* poster. Scene: "Red Plums are for the Eighth Army. Chairman Mao is the savior. The village is liberated." The formation of the Eighth Army marked the beginning of the formation of the Red Army. 30" x 21". $60 - $80

Peasant Leader Jiang Shuiying. Main character from Revolutionary Peking Opera *Long Jiang Song*, who was a leader among the peasant class. Ceramic statue. 4" x 3" x 11". $40 - $60

Single Red Army Dancer, Wu Qionghua. Character from the Modern Revolutionary Ballet *The Red Army Detachment of Women*, in which women whose husbands joined the Red Army decided to join the Red Army as well by forming a female detachment and fighting class enemies side by side with their men. According to Mao, "women hold up half of the sky." Ceramic statue. 3" x 3" x 13". $40 - $60

Red Army Soldier, Wu Qionghua, with class enemy, Nan Batian. Depicts a scene from the modern revolution ballet *The Red Army Detachment of Women*. Ceramic statue. 8" x 4" x 14". $40 - $60

Dual Red Army Detachment Soldiers. Scene from Modern Revolutionary Ballet *The Red Army Detachment of Women*. Ceramic statue. 11" x 4" x 15". $90 - $150

Red Detachment Soldier, from *The Red Army Detachment of Women*. Hong Changqing, Chinese Communist Party (CCP) Representative. Ceramic statue. 5" x 4" x 15". $40 - $60

Poster of the female leader Wu Qionghua, from *The Red Army Detachment of Women*. Shanghai
People's Publishing House, February 1971. Print on paper. 30" x 21". $80 - $100

Poster describing "young soldiers practicing," from *The Red Army Detachment of Women*.
Beijing People's Publishing House. Print on paper. 30" x 21". $80 - $100

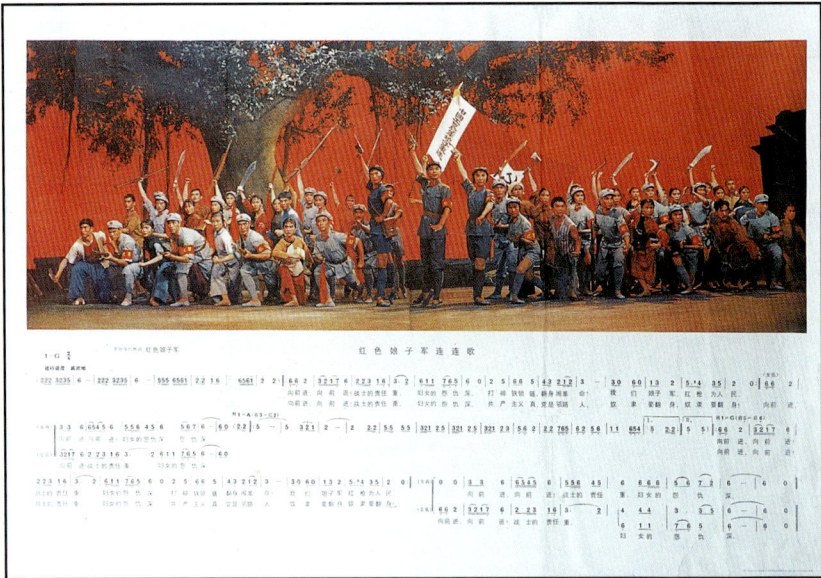

Poster with songs from *The Red Army Detachment of Women*. Tianjin People's Publishing House, February 1971. 0.14 Yuan. Print on paper. 30" x 21". $80-$120

Poster depicting a scene from *The Red Army Detachment of Women*: "The army and the people are as close as one family" with a song from the fourth scene's hat dance. Tianjin People's Art Publishing House, February 1971. 0.14 Yuan. Print on paper. 30" x 21". $80 - $100

Poster for *The Red Lantern*, a Revolutionary Peking Opera. The themes of the play include class struggle, the fight against Japanese invaders, and the Red Army's close connection to the people. In Chinese and Mongolian. Inner Mongolian People's Publishing House, May 1971. 0.10 Yuan. Print on paper. 30" x 21". $80 - $100

Li Yuhe, male lead character from *The Red Lantern*. Li Yuhe is a railroad worker and the son of a deceased Red Army soldier fighting the Japanese and the Nationalist Party. Ceramic statue. 3" x 3" x 10". $40 - $60

Li Tiemei, female lead character from *The Red Lantern*. Li Tiemei is a railroad worker and daughter of a deceased Red Army soldier. Ceramic statue. 3" x 3" x 10". $40 - $60

Poster depicting a scene from the Revolutionary Peking Opera *Taking Tiger Mountain by Strategy*. Yang Zirong solo from the eighth scene. Tianjin People's Art Publishing house, June 1971. 0.14 Yuan. Print on paper. 30" x 21". $80 - $100

胸有朝阳

Yang Zirong, lead character in the Revolutionary Peking Opera *Taking Tiger Mountain by Strategy*. Yang Zirong went underground to fight against the Nationalist Party in the Communist Revolution. Ceramic statue. 5" x 3" x 10". $40 - $60

Double-sided poster from *Taking Tiger Mountain by Strategy*.
People's Art Publishing House, Hebei Province, September
1990. 0.28 Yuan. Print on paper. 30" x 21". $80 - $100

Ah Ching Sao and Nationalist officials. Depicts a scene from the Modern Revolutionary Peking Opera *Sha Jia Bang*. Ah Ching Sao is a tea shop owner who secretly aids Red Army soldiers. In this scene she stalls Nationalist Party officials from searching for the Red Army soldiers in the tea shop while they make their escape. Hu Chunkui, Nationalist Party Captain, and Diao Deyi, Nationalist Party Lieutenant. Ceramic statue. 11" x 5" x 13". $80 - $150

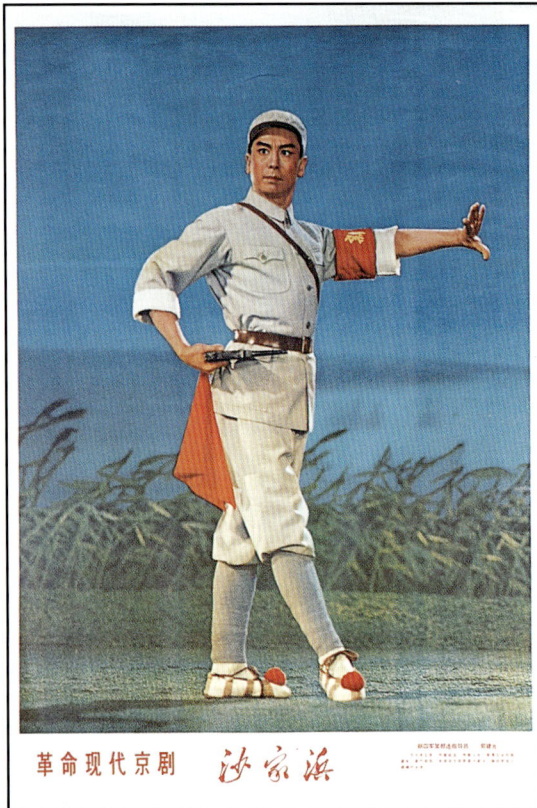

Modern Revolutionary Peking Opera *Sha Jia Bang*. New Fourth division army leader Guo Jiangang. Shanghai People's Publishing House, October 1970. 0.10 Yuan. Print on paper. 30" x 21". $80 - $100

Modern Revolutionary Peking Opera *Sha Jia Bang*. Poster of Ah Qing Sao, the heroine who opened a tea shop to provide a disguised location for meetings of Red Army officers. Inner Mongolia People's Publishing House, May 1971. 0.10 Yuan. Print on paper. 30" x 21". $80 - $100

Ah Ching Sao (Auntie Ah Ching).
Ceramic statue. 3" x 3" x 12". $40 - $60

Fang Haizhen, female lead character from the
Revolutionary Peking Opera *On the Docks*.
Ceramic statue. 4" x 3" x 10". $40 - $60

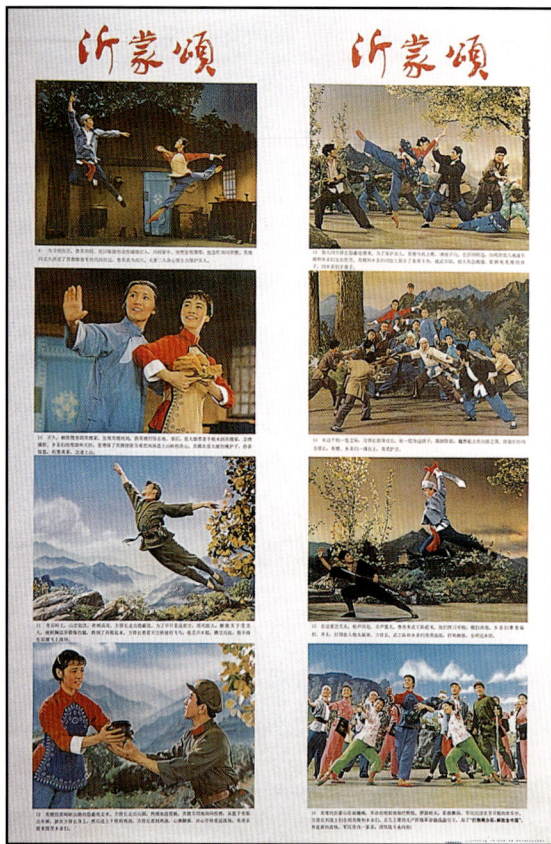

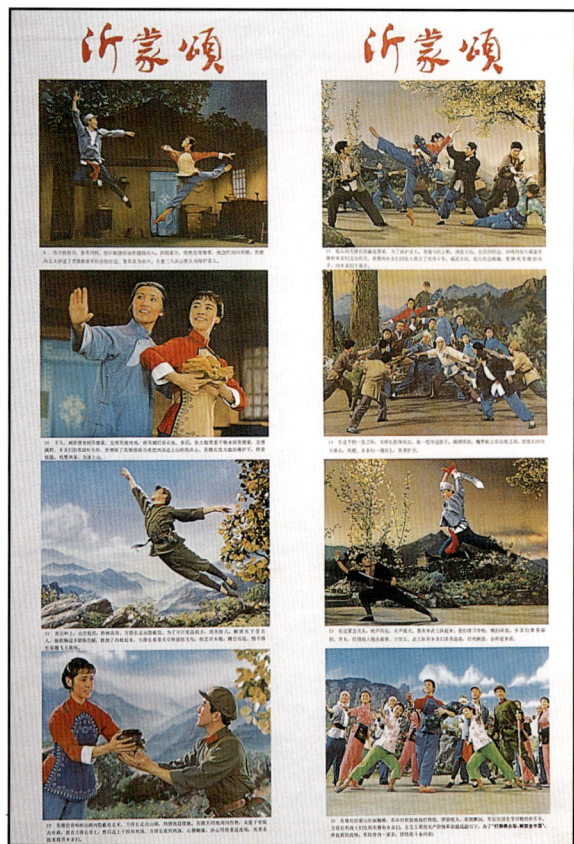

Double-sided poster for the Modern Revolutionary Peking Opera *Yin Mong Song,* performed by the People's Dance Group. People's Art Publishing House, July 1976. 0.28 Yuan. Print on paper. 30" x 21". 1,490,000 copies. $100 - $160

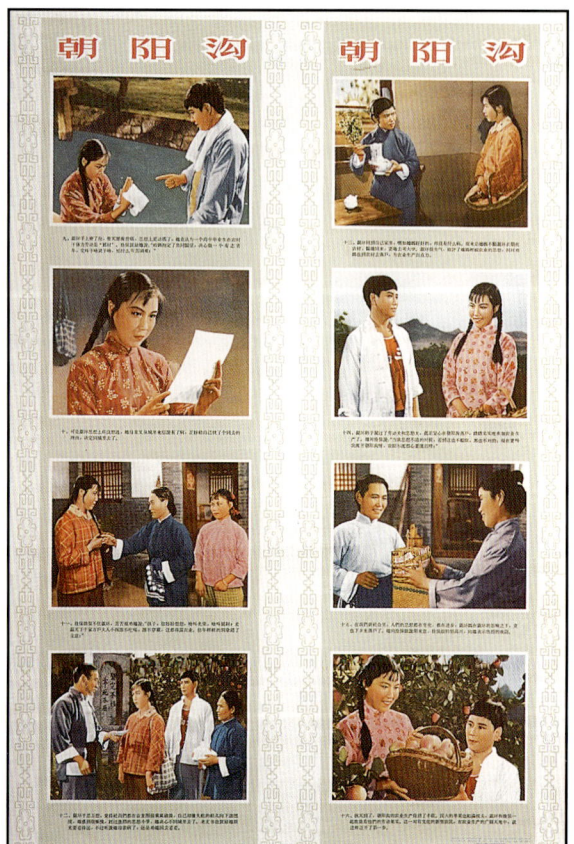

Double-sided movie poster from *Chang Yang Ge,* a story about a city woman finding love in the countryside and marrying a poor farmer. The movie was distributed to support and promote Mao's wish for city youth to go to the countryside and learn from the farmers by living and working with them side-by-side. Chinese Movie Publishing house, October 1964 (4th Edition, May 1966). 900,000 copies. 0.30 Yuan. Print on paper. 30" x 21". $100 - $160

Little young Red Guard emulating the heroine from the *Red Army Detachment of Women*. Ceramic statue. 3" x 3" x 10". $40 - $60

Poster for the Revolutionary Peking Opera *Lu Hua Dang*, with children performing. Tianjin People's Art publishing House. Printed by Hebei Foreign Trade Wrapping and Printing Company, June 1983. 0.18 Yuan. Print on paper. $80 - $100

"Education must serve the Great Proletarian Class, education must be integrated with production and field labor, the working class must be educated, and intellectuals must become proficient in field labor." Wuhan Revolutionary Committee, August 1968. Print on paper. 30" x 21". $60 - $80

Doctrine No. 2 – The broader world resides in the countryside – "Up to the Mountains and Down to the Villages."

In the years before and during the Cultural Revolution, approximately 13 million students, including Red Guards, were "sent down," forced to move to rural areas and live as peasants for the purpose of reeducation. Often only 15 or 16 years of age, they were not allowed to return home, even during holidays, and many ended up marrying and settling down where they were sent. Students who were not sent down spent most of their school time in the fields, working side by side with the peasants and eating peasant meals. Many who lived through these times wrote memoirs, collectively referred to as "scar literature," in the late 1970s and early 1980s.

The idealized version of the sending of students to the countryside included example villages such as Dazhai, where the students lived under simple peasant conditions and made significant contributions to the rural economy. In fact, one of the slogans for the sent down students was to have the Dazhai spirit. The "barefoot doctors," working on rural health issues under spartan conditions, figured prominently in this period.

"Establish roots in the factory and farm land." People's Police Protection of Mao Zedong Revolution Group. Wood block print on paper. 30" by 21". $60 - $80

"Great country, wide land, we can do what we want." Poster depicts the mass youth "sent down" program, in which urban youth were sent to the countryside to live and work. Wood block print on paper. 30" x 21". $60 - $80

Female farmer harvesting. Ceramic statue. 4.5" x 4" x 12". $40 - $60

Peasant woman. Ceramic statue. 3" x 4" x 11". $40 - $60

The barefoot doctor. Ceramic statue. 3" x 3" x 12". $50 - $70

Chinese minority woman. Ceramic statue. 4" x 3.4" x 9". $40 - $60

The barefoot doctor. Ceramic statue. 4" x 3" x 11". $50 - $70

A "sent down" youth. Ceramic statue.
3" x 3" x 13". $40 - $60

Two young "sent down" girls. Ceramic statue. 6" x 5.5" x 11".
$80 - $120

Happy celebration of the welcoming of a New Village
Commune Member. New Village Commune members
were the intellectual youth "sent down" to be re-
educated by farmers. Author Wang Xisong, member of
Shizuizan city's cultural center. Ningxia People's
Publishing House, August 1975. 0.11 Yuan. Print on
paper. 30" x 21". $60 - $80

探姐姐

Visiting Older Sister. Older sister refers to a sent-down youth. Author Li Jianhua. Shanghai People's Fine Art Publishing house, June 1978. 0.11 Yuan. Print on paper. 30" x 21". $60 - $80

长大我也当社员

I want to be village commune member when I grow up. Background banner reads "Welcome Sent-Down Youth." Huang Lisheng. People's Publishing House, April 1976. 0.11 Yuan. Print on paper. 30" x 21". 900,000 copies printed. $60 - $80

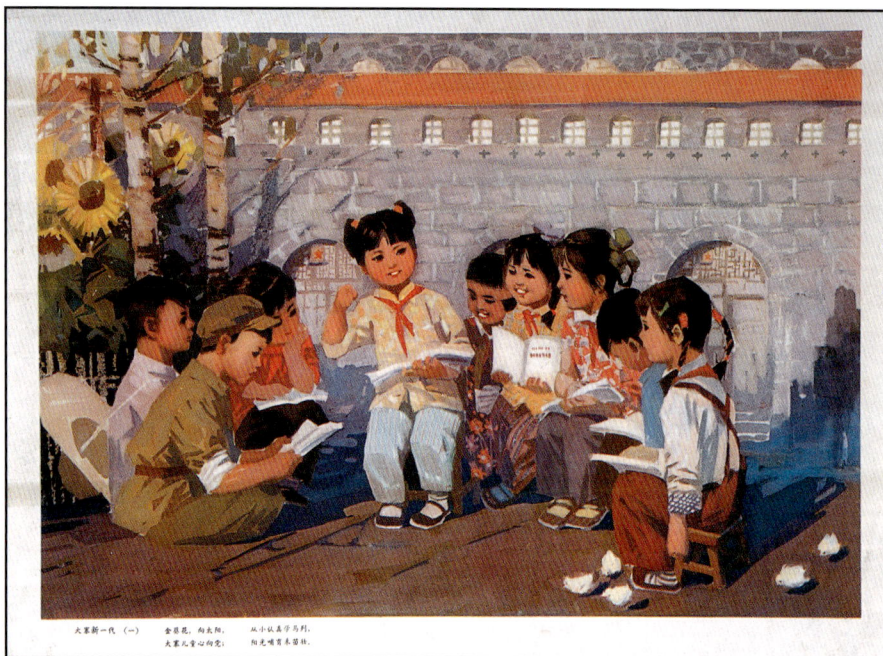

New generation in Dazhai. Elementary school educational poster, hung in classrooms and used to conduct political education. Reads: "sunflowers are facing the sun, and Dazhai's children's hearts are with the Communist Party." Dazhai's children study Marxism-Leninism, the sunlight grows a strong harvest. Print on paper. 30" x 21". $60 - $80

Walking the Dazhai path starting from a young age. Small standing board indicating that students from Yanan elementary school were building a model agricultural field. Liu Changgui, a student from Beijing Normal School Revolution Drama division. Elementary school students Beijing People Publishing House, November 1975. 0.14 Yuan. Print on paper. 30" x 21". $60 - $80

The entire party promotes agricultural education and strives to broadly implement "Dazhai." Beijing City Movie Production Company movie listing on agricultural educational themed films poster. November 1975. Print on paper. 30" x 21". $60 - $80

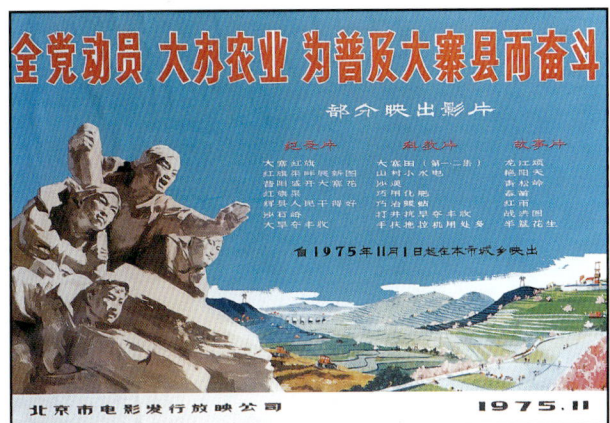

The background reads "Down with Gang of Four" and "Unity under Chairman Hua Guofeng." Dazhai was a model village created during Cultural Revolution for all villages. Artist Wu Li. People's Publishing House, 1977. 0.14 Yuan. Print on paper. $60 - $80

Doctrine No. 3 – The main force for the revolution belongs to the workers, peasants, and soldiers. "Learn from workers, peasants, and soldiers."

Mao had directed that the working class leads the revolution, and that the workers, peasants, and PLA soldiers were the elite vanguard of the revolutionary movement. Building on this, the government instituted the "Learn from workers, peasants, and soldiers" movement. Statues and posters were made to demonstrate idealized examples of the revolutionary classes.

Unity of peasant, factory worker and PLA soldier (three main proletarian classes). Ceramic statue. 11" x 5" x 15". $160 - $200

Red Army soldier and guerilla. Ceramic statue. 9" x 3" x 11".
$90 - $150

Steel worker. Ceramic statue. 4" x 3" x 13".
$40 - $60

PLA soldier Dong Cunrui. Dong Cunrui was a heroic party member, who died during a battle against the Nationalist Party during the Chinese Civil War (1946 – 1949). Dong placed an explosive charge on a bridge and held it until exploded, allowing the Red Army to advance and sacrificing himself in the process. Ceramic statue. 3" x 3" x 13". $40 - $60

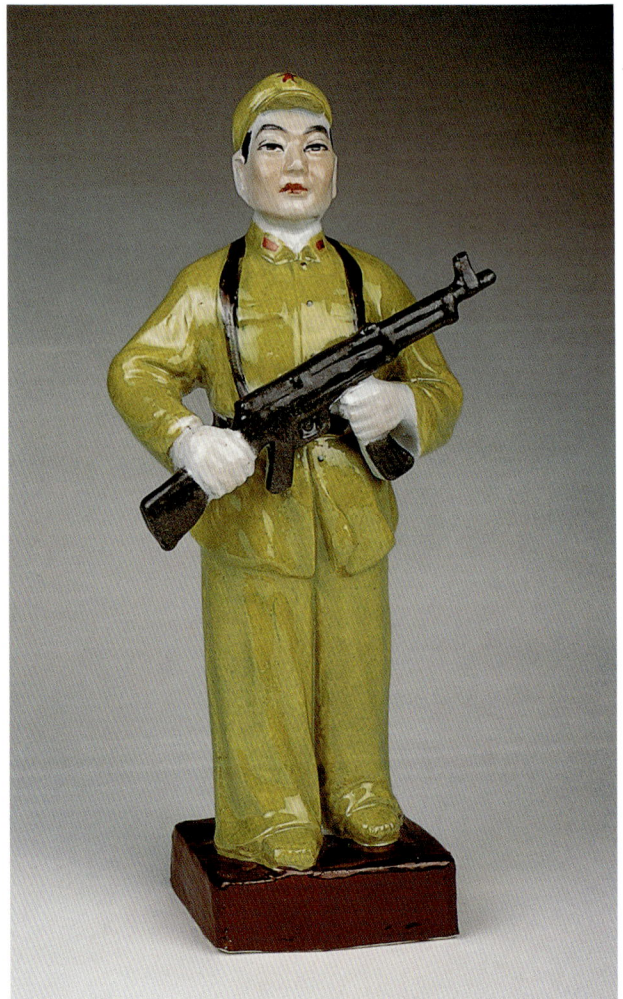

PLA soldier. Ceramic statue. 3.5" x 3.3" x 11.5". $40 - $60

Red Army soldier. Ceramic statue. 3" x 3" x 12".
$40 - $60

PLA soldier. Ceramic statue. 3.5" x 3.5" x 11".
$40 - $60

Female Scarlet Guard. During the Communist Revolution Scarlet Guards worked with the Red Army as guerilla soldiers. Mao said of revolutionary armies that they "move among the people like a fish in water." Ceramic statue. 3" x 3" x 11".
$40 - $60

Female National Guard soldier.
Ceramic statue. 3.5" x 3.5" x 11".
$40 - $60

Island Home Guard. Ceramic statue. 4" x 4" x 15".
$40 - $60

PLA female field phone operator.
Ceramic statue. 3" x 3" x 12". $50 - $70

Red Army soldier, soldier from before the formation of the PLA. Ceramic statue. 4" x 5" x 11". $40 - $60

Chinese People's Volunteer Force soldier, who came to the aid of North Korea against the United States during the Korean War. Ceramic statue. 5" x 4" x 14". $50 - $70

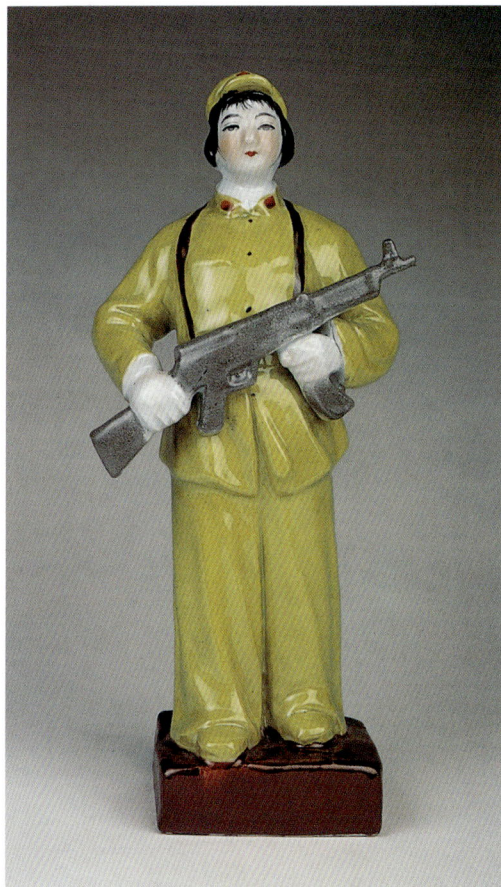

Female PLA soldier. Ceramic statue. 3" x 3" x 14". $40 - $60

Red Army soldier. Ceramic statue. 3.5" x 3.5" x 12".
$40 - $60

Small Sewing Needle Pack. A common saying was that one
should inherit the Red Army soldier's ways by not throwing
away things that one could fix. Poster developed for kindergar-
ten children. Liang Hongtao, artist. Shanghai educational
department, December 1978. 50,000 copies printed. Print on
paper. 0.06 Yuan. $60 - $80

We are all good shots. Depiction of young women from the outer islands of
China holding and cleaning their rifles. Zhao Shuqin. People's Art Publishing
house, December 1975 (first ed.). 165,000 copies printed. 0.07 Yuan. Print on
paper. 21" x 15". $60 - $80

"The entire party focuses on military affairs." "Three Defenses" poster. Chinese People's Liberation Army Central Chief of Staff Political Department. Print on paper. 30" x 21". $60 - $80

Battlefield wedding. A woman getting married to her PLA soldier husband who's on duty in the field. Li Hongquan, artist. Sichuan Art publishing house, June 1987. Print on paper. $60 - $80

我们也去打靶

"Going to Target Practice." Children meet with a national guard to learn marksmanship. Sun Jiayao, artist. Hebei People's Publishing House, October 1975. 310,000 copies. 0.14 Yuan. Print on paper. 30" x 21". $60 - $80

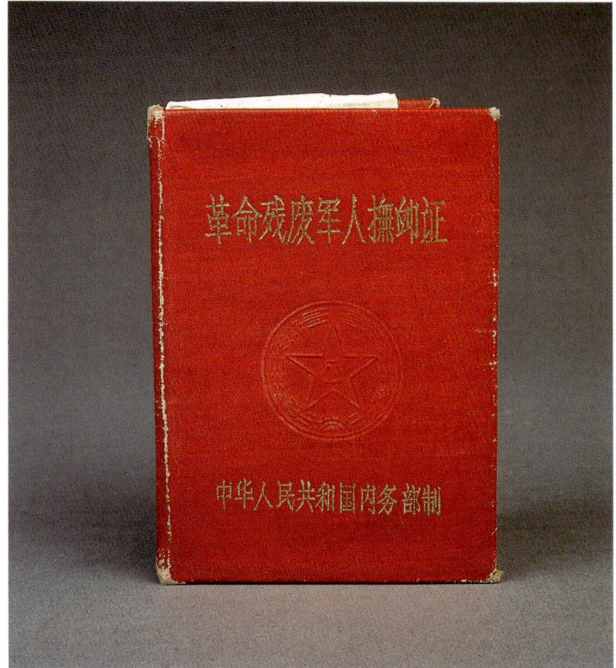

革命残废军人抚卹证

中华人民共和国内务部制

Disabled worker certificate. Entitled holder to government benefits for Chi Jinggui, with stamps indicating the benefits that were given and received. December 1962. $30 - $50

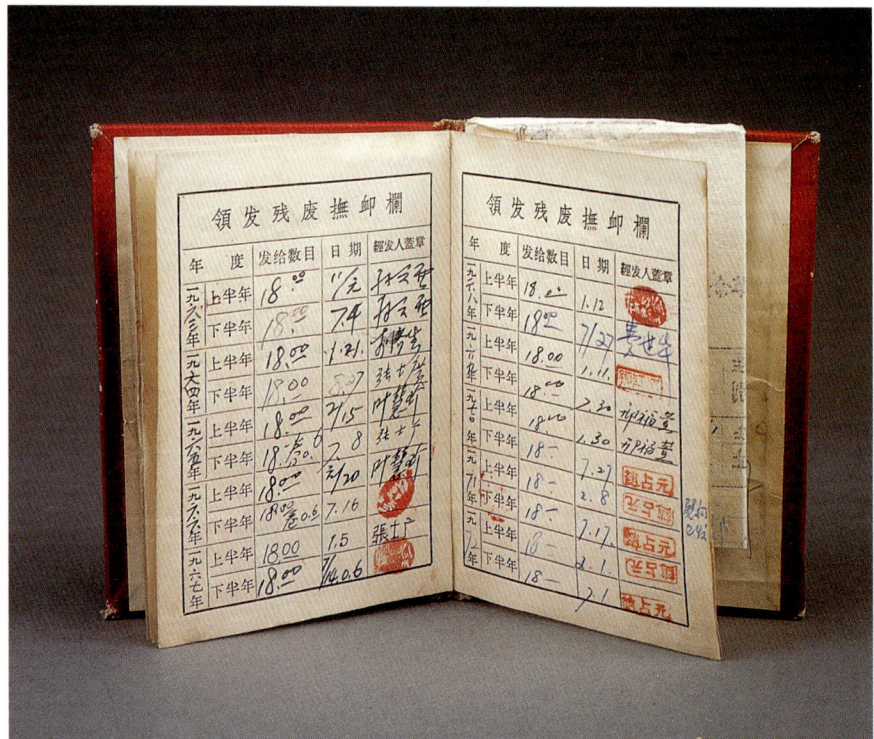

Doctrine No. 4 – The Nationalist Party is a Class enemy, Taiwanese people are living a hellish life on earth, and we must liberate Taiwan to save the people from the suppression of the Nationalist Party.

As the Cultural Revolution lost momentum, the government focused the attention of the Chinese people on other "enemies" (other than class enemies). Taiwan and Vietnam began to figure prominently in propaganda posters, encouraging the Chinese people to work hard to support the struggle against the "ruling class" in these regions. Other posters demonstrated the people's resolve to "liberate" Taiwan, including images of children preparing care packages to be sent to Taiwan. After the Vietnam War in the 1960s and early 1970s, Vietnam and China had a falling out over policy in Southeast Asia, especially Cambodia and China's support of Pol Pot. This tension culminated in the invasion of Vietnam by China (which the Chinese government characterized as an invasion by Vietnam). Although many of these posters had been produced earlier, they began to gain prominence as the government shifted attention away from internal political campaigns.

一定要解放台湾！

"We Must Liberate Taiwan." Developed by Nanjing Chinese PLA air force, Red Eagle Creative Team. Shanghai People's Art Publishing House. 0.12 Yuan. Stamped "invalidated." Print on paper. 31" x 21". $60 - $80

"We must liberate Taiwan!" Developed by Chinese Air force Red Eagle Creative Team. Central Command Printing Company, September 1970. 0.08 Yuan. Wood block print on paper. 31" x 21". $60 - $80

我们一定要解放台湾

Letter to the little friends of Taiwan. Shows gifts to be sent by mainland Chinese children to Taiwanese children. Letter excerpt indicates that the children wish that Taiwan would be united with the Motherland of China. In the foreground is a picture titled "I love Tiananmen". Created by Xie Congrong and Ling Yongquan. Print on paper. 30" x 21". $60 - $80

Chinese rocket ceramic statue. A male factory worker and a female peasant riding on the rocket holding a sign that reads "exceed US and UK," a slogan coined during the Great Leap Forward. Ceramic statue. 14" x 5" x 14". $200 - $400

Doctrine No. 5 – Capitalists and Imperialists must be defeated

Another set of enemies re-emphasized in the latter part of the Cultural Revolution were the rivals of China on the international stage, especially the United States and United Kingdom. Earlier images of the Great Leap Forward such as the Chinese rocket statue featuring the slogan of the 1950s era, "Exceed U.S. and UK" were reintroduced in ceramic statues. After the Sino-Soviet split in the 1960s, Mao branded the Soviet Union as another "Capitalist" country, along countries such as the United States and United Kingdom. Although U.S.-China relations were normalized in 1972, the internal campaigns did not cease entirely.

As part of its campaign against imperialist and capitalist countries, China positioned itself as the leader of the Third World. Propaganda posters depicted China uniting other countries in Latin America, Asia and Africa were abundant. Often showing people's resolve, marching forward together, the posters of this period were often more graphically violent than others. Posters from the early 1950s showing a struggle against external class enemies were reintroduced in this period, along with new posters reflecting China's new allies and adversaries and distributed to show the Chinese people's tenacity against outside enemies. A significant change, however, came in the fact that China shifted from following the Soviet Union's lead to forming the vanguard itself.

"American Invaders will be Defeated!" This poster depicts two People's Liberation Army soldiers, each holding a book. The book on the left reads "Soviet Army Defeated 1,200,000 German Nazi, Italian, Japanese and other countries' soldiers during World War Two." The right book reads "Chinese People's Liberation Army defeated 8 million soldiers from American Imperialist-sponsored Chiang Kai-Chek army." On the bottom section of the poster, it depicts defeated Americans holding a dollar sign flag, and in writing it states "Next year we can accumulate 3 million soldiers." Printed in July 1951. In the early fifties, poster still used traditional Chinese characters, and some of the words were printed from right to left. Print on paper. $300 - $500

People of the world will come together! Down with American capitalism, and down with Soviet hegemony! Small print reads "Strong support to Asian, African and Latin American people's righteous struggle against America!" and "Strong support to Arabic people's righteous struggle against America!" Created and submitted by Shanghai Mao Theory Advocacy Team to the Central Art and Craft School's *Jing-Gang-Shang* Red Guards. Xinhua Publishing House, Shanghai, August 1969. 0.18 Yuan. Print on paper. 16" x 32". $150 - $300

"Attack the Invader." Movie poster for Sino-Vietnamese War. Print on paper. $80 - $150

Down with the new emperor (*Xin Sha Huang*). The new emperor is a reference to the Soviet Union. This poster appeared after the Sino-Soviet split. Print on paper. $80 - $120

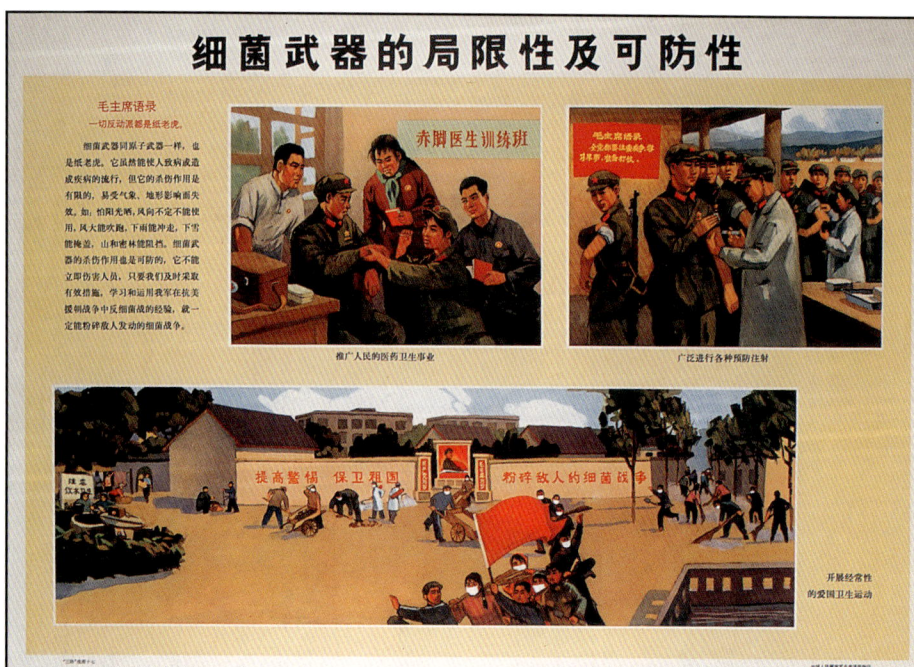

Biochemical weapon's limitation and prevention. The poster features Mao's excerpt that coined the phrase of "paper tiger," in that it says "All counter revolutionaries are Paper Tigers." It also shows a Barefoot Doctor giving shots to PLA soldiers. The bottom half of the poster image shows a wall with the following words: "Raise Alert level, Protect the Country, and Destroy Enemy's Biochemical Warfare." Chinese People's Liberation Army Chief of Staff Department. Print on paper. $60 - $80

Doctrine No. 6 – Learn from Comrade Lei Feng

Lei Feng, a name familiar to all Chinese, represents the selfless spirit that the communist government encourages in its citizens. Lei Feng's story varies depending on whom you ask. The official version was that he was a PLA soldier who started life as an orphan and sacrificed himself for the good of the people. When he died he left behind volumes of diaries detailing his study of Mao and many sacrifices for his fellow soldiers and civilians.

The unauthorized version is a little less heroic. When Lei was orphaned soon after the revolution, other residents of his village adopted him but could not accept his habits of stealing and making mischief. He was sent to northeast China to serve as a soldier. One day in 1962 while on an errand, he drove into a telephone pole and died. The diaries and acts of selflessness were supposedly all fabricated by the government to provide an ideological poster boy.

Whether true or not, the story of Lei Feng was widely disseminated. Mao urged the nation in 1963 to "Learn from Comrade Lei Feng" and initiated the campaign of learning from Lei to become a "little screw in the revolutionary machine," not very fancy but very useful. The campaign promoted Lei's self-sacrificing spirit, putting the country, the Party and others before oneself and becoming loyal guardians of the Party. The most productive campaign results came from school-age students, who widely accepted the Lei Feng campaign and worked widely to help elders and others. In the early 1970s, with Mao withdrawing from propaganda, Lei became a proxy for Mao. After the Tiananmen Square Incident in 1989, the government once more posted Lei Feng images widely in an effort to focus the Chinese people on their common interests and away from recent events.

"Learn from Lei Feng." Ma Hongdao, artist. Jiangxi Art Publishing House. 0.50 Yuan. Print on paper. $60 - $80

向雷锋同志学习

"Learn from Comrade Lei Feng and Serve the People wholeheartedly." Ni Fanghua, artist. Jiangxi Art Publishing House. 0.50 Yuan. Print on paper. $60 - $80

学习雷锋好榜样
全心全意为人民服务

"Learn from Comrade Lei Feng's good example and Love the Socialist Society and the People." Qiu Wei, artist. Jiangxi Art Publishing House. 0.50 Yuan. Print on paper. $60 - $80

PLA soldier Northeastern division (in cold weather gear). Inscription on base reads "Learn from Comrade Lei Feng." Ceramic statue. $40 - $60

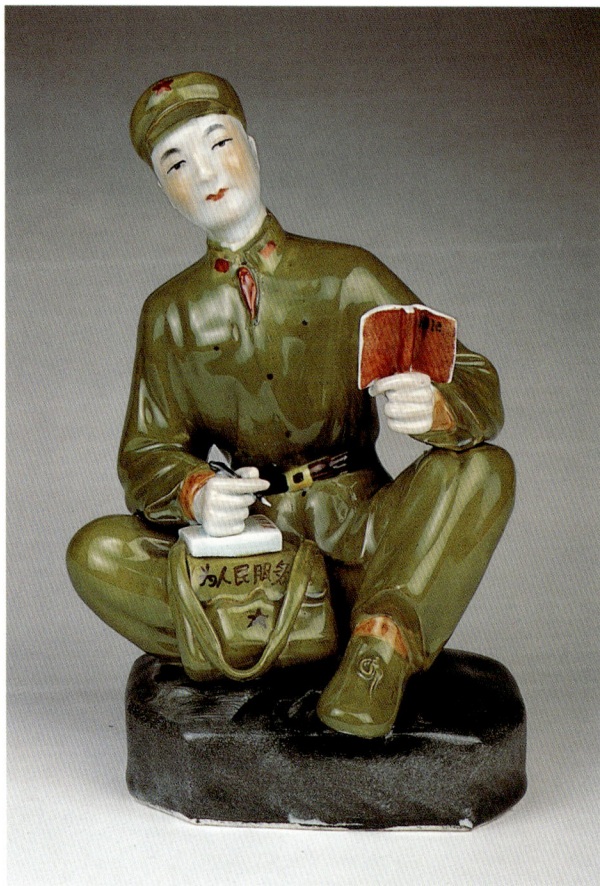

Lei Feng and his diary. Ceramic statue. $80 - $120

"Learn from Comrade Lei Feng, be a loyal soldier to the mother country." Wang Xinbin and Cao Shuqin, artists. Shanxi Military Political Cultural Department. Liaoning Art Publishing House. Print on paper. $60 - $80

学习雷锋同志 做祖国的忠诚卫士

"Spread Lei Feng Spirit, Walk Lei Feng's Path." Wang Xinbin and Cao Shuqin, artists. Liaoning Province Political Cultural Department. Liaoning Art Publishing House. Print on paper. $60 - $80

弘扬雷锋精神 走雷锋成长道路

Lei Feng's words - To live is to make other people's lives better. Dong Chensheng, artist. People's Education Publishing House Political Department. People's Education Publishing House, Beijing, 1984. Print on paper. $60 - $80

自己活着，就是为了使别人过得更美好。 雷锋

Learn to count (7). Depiction of politically correct behavior combined with a math lesson for school-children. The counting is related to how many children are helping the older lady, widow of a veteran. Shanghai elementary class educational material, first grade math class. Print on paper. $50 - $70

Learn to Count (4). Depiction of four children cleaning their classrooms, model student behavior. First grade math class. Print on paper. $50 - $70

Helping Old Grandma. Elementary school educational poster. Print on paper. $50 - $70

Little Precious Looking for her mother. (With the help of PLA soldiers and other common citizens.) Elementary school educational material. Print on paper. $50 - $70

Giving seat (basic training) elementary school
classroom material. Ha Qiongwen. Shanghai
Education Department. Print on paper. $50 - $70

Learn from Comrade Lei Feng, and always do
things for the people. Poster reads "People's
life is limited, but the spirit of serving people
goes on forever." Print on paper. $60 - $80

146

向雷锋同志学习

Learn from Comrade Lei Feng with Mao Zedong's calligraphy. After the massacre in Tiananmen Square in 1989, propaganda posters featuring Lei Feng were re-introduced by the Chinese central government in an attempt to re-assert the authority of the Communist Party by emphasis on past campaigns. This poster was printed shortly after the incident in an attempt to reacquaint people with the self sacrificing spirit of the Communist Revolution. People's Art Publishing House, distributed by Beijing Bookstore in April 1990. 0.85 Yuan. Print on paper. $60 - $80

Aside from Lei Feng, other heroes and martyrs existed either in real life or in propaganda films such as Huang Jiguang, Yang Gensi, Liu Wenxue, and Sisters from the Big Steppes (from a movie titled *Sisters from the Big Steppes*), and Pan Dongzi (a little heroic boy from the movie of *Sparkling Red Star*), etc. Their images were widely shown in posters, statues or film formats. The theme was consistent – do what the party asks and do not hesitate to sacrifice.

Pang Dongzi. 1976 calendar featuring Pang Dongzi, a movie character. A brave young child who fought the Japanese invaders during World War II, and was killed by an abusive landowner who had allied himself with the Japanese invaders. The background of the poster shows a child holding a book on Lei Feng. Qi Daoyan and Dan Lianxiao, artists. Dalian Electrical Ceramic Company. People's Art Publishing House, October 1976. 500,000 copies. 0.07 Yuan. Print on paper. $60 - $80

"Not to be Destroyed Road." Scene from the Korean War. The Chinese PLA soldier wears a tag that reads "Chinese People's Volunteer Army,"; referring to soldiers who were sent to fight with the North Koreans against South Korea and the U.S. Army. Dai Qinglu and Wang Zhenjia. People's Liberation Army Chief of Staff Political Department, June, 1973. Print on paper. $60 - $80

Yang Gensi. Korean war hero from China. Used as a textbook insert for elementary school education program. Shanghai People's publishing house, June 1974. 0.16 Yuan. Print on paper. 225,000 copies. $60 - $80

Huang Jiguang. Korean war hero from China. Huang Jiguang, a soldier whose task was to bomb a U.S. Army pillbox, died in the effort. Poster used in conjunction with elementary Chinese textbook. Zhang Hongzan, artist. Shanghai Education Publishing House, c.1975. Print on paper. $60 - $80

Liu Wenxue. A Young Pioneer student declared a hero who allegedly died while fighting with a land owner who had stolen food from the people's commune. Ceramic statue. 4" x 3" x 13". $40 - $60

Sister from the Steppe. From the story "the Sisters from the Steppe", about Mongolian children who worked to save sheep from a storm to provide them to the party. Ceramic statue. 7" x 5" x 11". $60 - $80

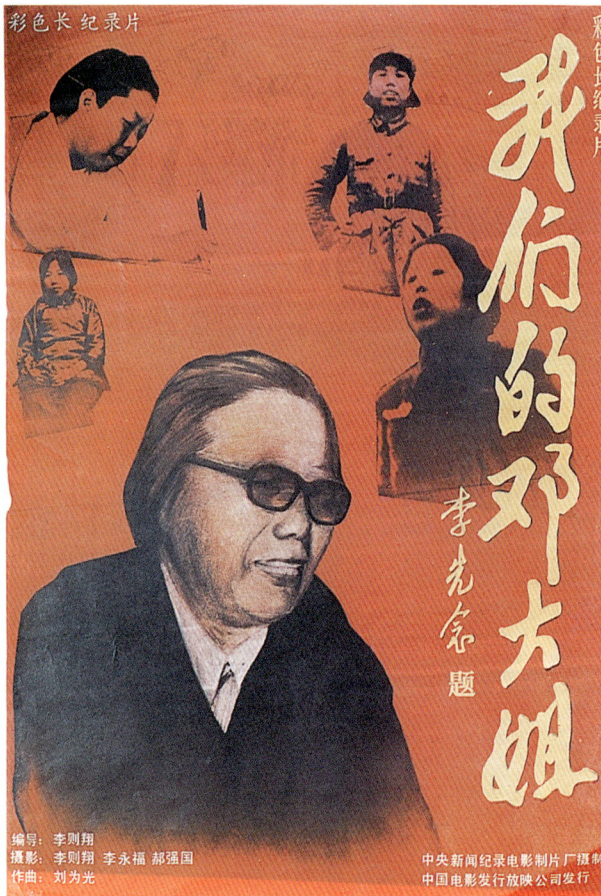

Our big sister Deng. Movie poster in memory of Zhou Enlai's wife, Deng Yingchao. She was known to have sacrificed herself for the good of the country by not having children and thought of as the "older sister" to the Chinese Children. It was said she and Zhou could never conceive. China News Documentary Production Company. Print on paper. $40 - $60

Chapter 9
New Focus, New Era

In October 1976, the members of the Gang of Four, the most active leaders of the Cultural Revolution, were arrested. They were put on trial and sentenced to death or life imprisonment. Mao's successor, Hua Guofeng, remained in power only a short while and was succeeded by Deng Xiaoping in 1978.

Under Deng's leadership, the country embarked on a campaign to build a socialist state with Chinese characteristics. The propaganda art during this period reflects a renewed energy toward positive accomplishments, such as world peace, personal hygiene and health care, population control, traditional values, and patriotism.

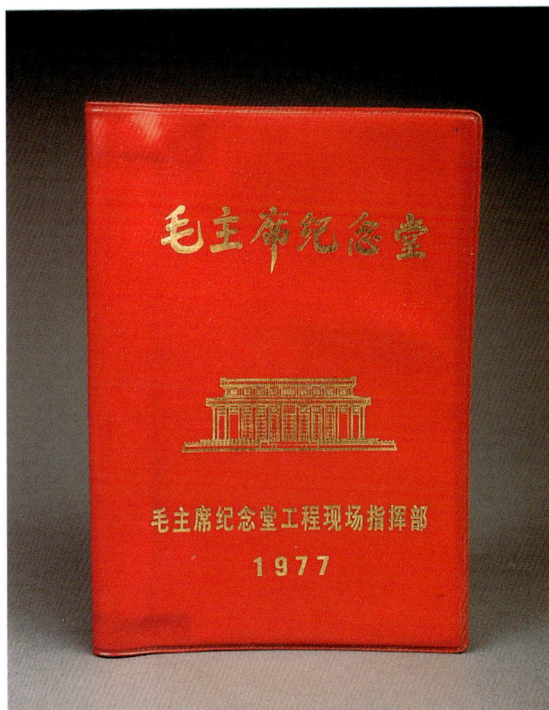

毛主席纪念堂

毛主席纪念堂工程现场指挥部

1977

Mao Zedong Memorial Certificate. Distributed only to the headquarters of the Mao Zedong Memorial construction project commemorating the completion of the Mao Mausoleum. 1977. $40 - $60

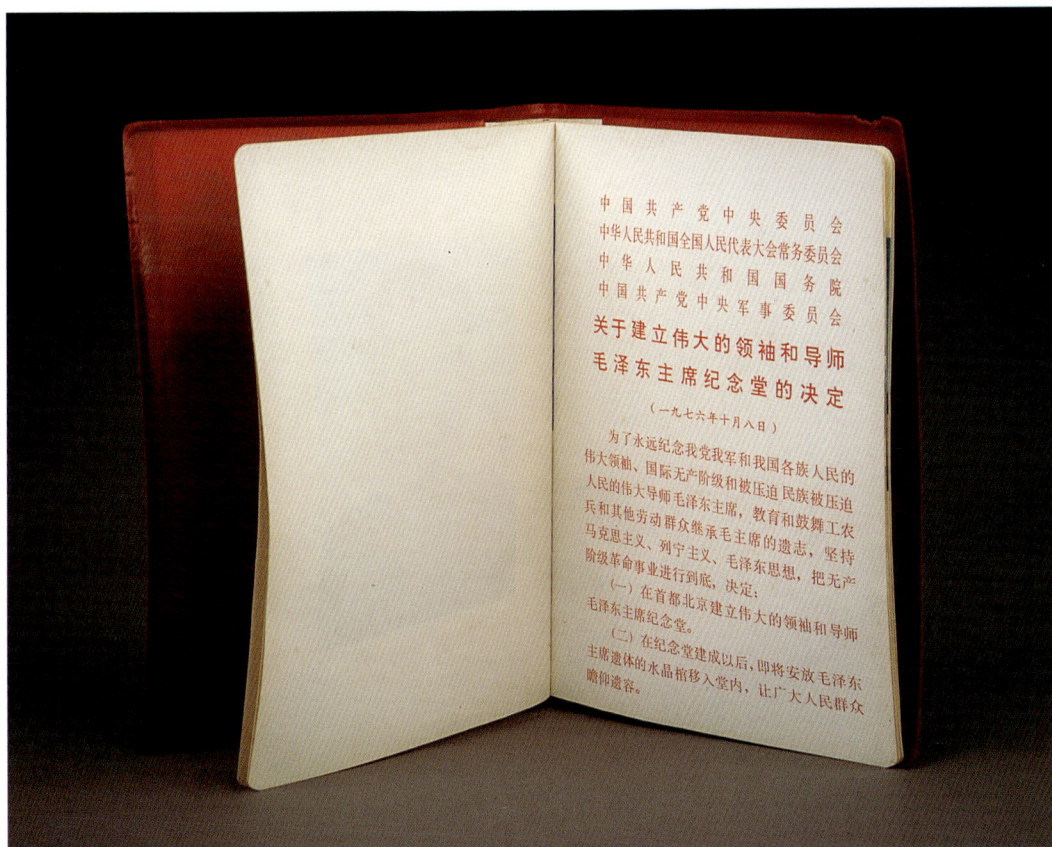

中 国 共 产 党 中 央 委 员 会
中华人民共和国全国人民代表大会常务委员会
中 华 人 民 共 和 国 国 务 院
中 国 共 产 党 中 央 军 事 委 员 会

关于建立伟大的领袖和导师
毛泽东主席纪念堂的决定

(一九七六年十月八日)

为了永远纪念我党我军和我国各族人民的伟大领袖、国际无产阶级和被压迫民族被压迫人民的伟大导师毛泽东主席,教育和鼓舞工农兵和其他劳动群众继承毛主席的遗志,坚持马克思主义、列宁主义、毛泽东思想,把无产阶级革命事业进行到底,决定:

(一)在首都北京建立伟大的领袖和导师毛泽东主席纪念堂。

(二)在纪念堂建成以后,即将安放毛泽东主席遗体的水晶棺移入堂内,让广大人民群众瞻仰遗容。

贈給上山下乡知识青年家长

北京市革命委员会

一九七七年二月

你 办 事，我 放 心。

Mao Zedong and Hua Guofeng. Famous image associated with a comment by Mao regarding Hua: "With you in charge, I will not have to worry." Hua was hand picked by Mao as his successor, but senior cadres ousted him during the Communist Party Third Plenum in December 1978, blaming him for economic setbacks and a lack of political and organizational ability. This event marked Deng Xiaoping's move to power, along with the reform-minded Hu Yaobang. Same image was used to produce millions of different themed posters. The first poster was given to families of intellectual youth who had been "sent down" (relocated to the countryside for reeducation). The second was given to veterans, veterans' families and families of martyrs by the Inner Mongolian Revolutionary Committee. c.1977 $60 - $80

華国锋主席在天安门城楼上向参加庆祝大会的首都百万军民亲切招手致意

人民美术出版社　　　1977年9月　定价0.20元

Chairman Hua Guofeng at Tiananmen Square. People's Fine Art Publishing,
September 1977. 0.20 Yuan. Print on paper. $60 - $80

Hua Guofeng with minority community leaders. Poster was given to single child
families by Hebei provincial planning reproduction office in 1980. $60 - $80

河北省计划生育办公室赠 一九八〇年

赠给独生子女家庭

Ration coupons were a common item from the founding of the People's Republic of China until well into the 1980s. As in the Soviet Union and the United States during World War II, food and other consumer goods were in short supply and had to be allocated through ration coupons issued by the government.[7] The Cultural Revolution exacerbated what had already been a tight supply, as the productive resources of the economy were directed to political campaigns and other relatively unproductive activities.

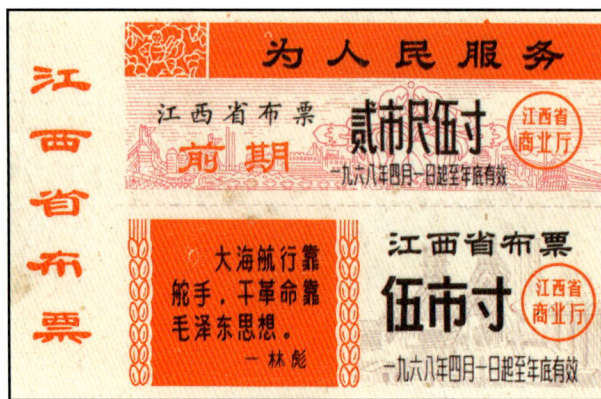

Provincial Fabrics Ration stamps. Ration Stamps were used to purchase fabrics in a controlled economy, with expiration date and the quantity, as well as the province it originated from. Some also contain Mao's thoughts on them. Bottom two consist of ration stamps for cotton from Guizhou province and Ningxia province. Various sizes. $5 - $10 each

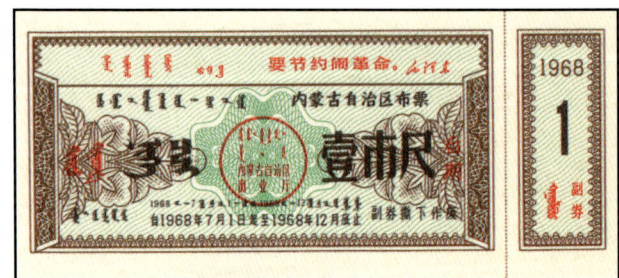

Provincial Cotton Certificates. Used to purchase cotton. Various sizes.

Provincial Food Ration stamps. Food Rations stamps were issued by individual provinces, some with working class people' pictures, some contain Mao's Words. All specify commodity, quantity, the year and province of issuance. Various sizes. $5 - $15 each

安徽省革命委员会

毛泽东思想学习班学员食堂

早　餐　券

丢失不补　过期作废

一、饭票只限本食堂使用，不作货币流通。

（12）

二、饭票应慎加爱护，涂抹作废。

（12）

★食堂饭票★

（壹1万2圆）

10000元　1953 7.印　10000元

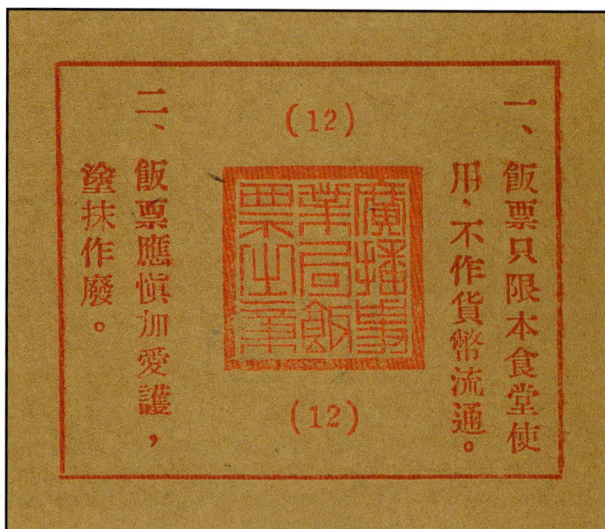

Local cafeteria meal ticket. State owned government enterprises cafeteria meal tickets to purchase rice, yam and other basic foods. Various sizes. $5 - $10 each

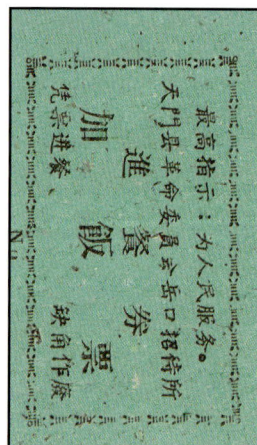

最高指示

千万不要忘

记阶级斗争

米　肆两

济南印刷厂革命委员会食堂

地　瓜

只限对内专用对外无效

1969年8月日

粗粮　2两

安阳农业勤城厂食堂

最高指示

人民，只有人民，才是创造世界历史的动力。

济南印刷厂革命委员会食堂

菜票

只限本食堂使用　1969年1月印

最高指示：为人民服务。

天门县革命委员会安口招待所

加　进　餐券

凭票用餐　无票作废

武汉市永丰农工商综合服务公司
奖售肉票
叁斤
奖
1984年

2 西安市切面专用票 2
弐市斤 1983
全年通用　年终作废

沙市商食品公司
专章
鸡
壹只
凭票供应　遗失不补

吉林省线票
壹轴(支) 1979
副券撕下作废
副券 1

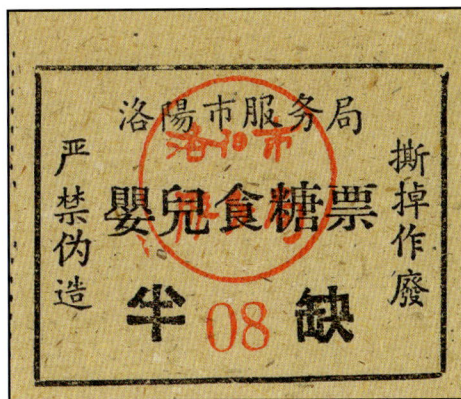

洛阳市服务局
严禁伪造
婴儿食糖票
撕掉作废
半 08 缺

派购鲜蛋结帐票
贰两
一九八四年有效

1 四平市粮食局居民食油供应票
豆油
壹公斤
1987

安徽省商业厅
奖售专用
香烟票
壹包
(只服本县市内使用)
日期：一九六四年八月一日
至一九六四年十二月底止

0.5 四平市粮食局居民食油供应票
葵花油
500克
1987

157

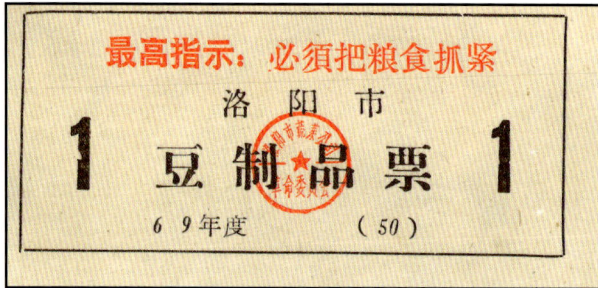

Ration stamp for animal fodder from Anhui province. Various sizes. $5 - $10 each

Coal Ration stamp from Jinan city. 3" x 1". $5 - $10 each

City Ration stamps. Used under the controlled economy for a variety of food groups such as meat, chicken, eggs, cigarettes, noodles, sugar, cooking oil and soy bean based products. Various sizes. $5 - $10 each

Ration stamp for gasoline for the People's Liberation Army. 5" x 3". $5 - $10 each

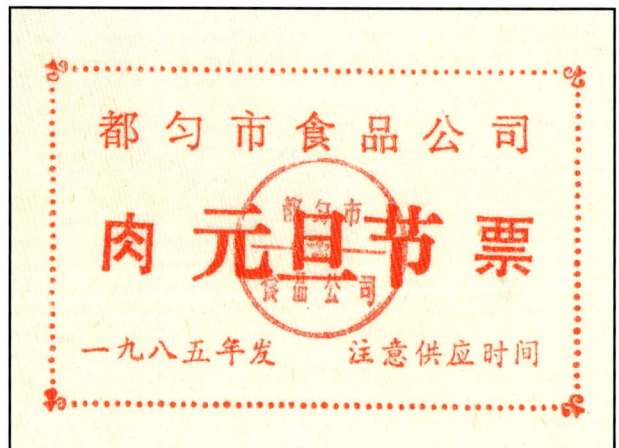

Holiday Ration stamp for meat products. Ration tickets for traditional holiday foods. Various sizes. $5 - $10 each

都匀市食品公司
肉 国庆节 票
一九八五年发　注意供应时间

都匀市食品公司
肉 五一节 票
一九八五年发　注意供应时间

都匀市食品公司
肉 春节 票
一九八五年发　注意供应时间

上海市粮食合同定购
化肥票
尿素
壹公斤
定点供应　隔年作废
1988

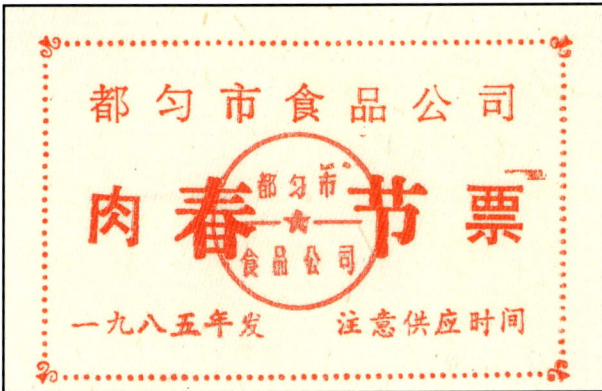

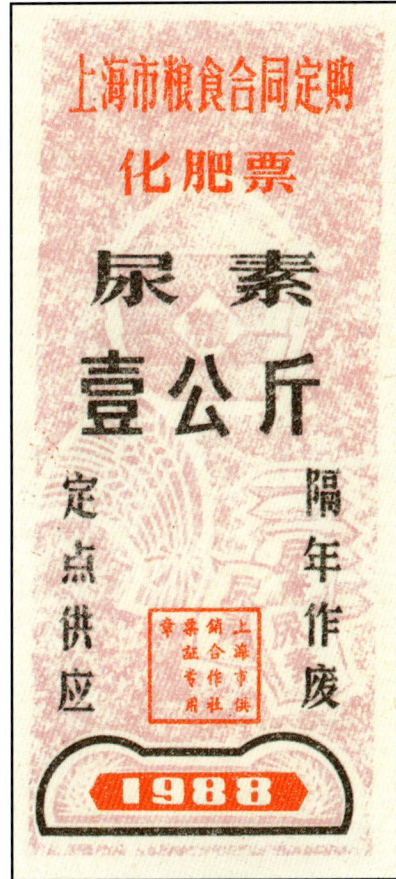

Fertilizer Ration stamp. 2" x 3". $5 - $10 each

Focus 1: World Peace and Unity.

World peace: After all the campaigns, the Chinese felt discouraged and numb about any political affairs. More peaceful images started to show up in the propaganda materials. Posters showing children of different races started to appear, which served the purposes of both portraying China as a multi-ethnic nation, and establishing its credentials as leader of the Third World against the capitalist and imperialist powers. It was during the late 70s and early 80s that this intent took on more peaceful expressions.

Public health and personal hygiene has always been problematic in China. Even as early as the 1920s, the founding father of China, Sun Yatsen, had advocated personal hygiene as a way of promoting good health and gaining national respect from foreign countries. In the late 1970s and early 1980s, personal hygiene was again an important national priority as a way of gaining prominence in the world as a civilized and cultured society. Cleaning was a big topic of these posters. During the Cultural Revolution, artists who created these health-related propaganda materials were often afraid of leaving any important political message behind, or not leaving enough of the important political message. As a result some posters would declare that one must take care of one's hygiene for the sake of revolution, but by the late 1970s or early 1980s, these posters were no longer dominated by revolutionary messages.

Our Mother Country is so Beautiful and Strong. Elementary school classroom environment wall hanging. Shi Qiren. Shanghai Education department. Print on paper. $50 - $70

The friendship flower blossoms. This Cultural Revolution propaganda poster depicts three children of different races, symbolizing world peace and unity. Shi Fuguo. Shanghai People's Art Publishing House, September 1978. 0.14 Yuan. Print on paper. $60 - $80

160

The earliest birth control-themed posters showed up during the Cultural Revolution, when in the early 1970s women were urged to marry later, and to have babies at a later age. In the early 1980s, the one-child policy took on momentum. Usually an image of a woman was depicted, with the slogan "fewer births will produce higher quality children."

Focus 2: Public Health and Safety, One Child Policy.

With the focus on the one-child policy, the importance of children in society was strengthened, if nothing else because they became scarcer. Coupled with the refocusing of people's energy from conducting struggle to taking care of their young children, posters developed by artists for school and children's holiday purposes appeared in abundance during the early to mid-1980s. In this new political environment, artists painting children exercising as part of extracurricular activities were able to paint without fear of conveying a non-revolutionary message.

I'll wash my little handkerchief. Personal hygiene poster. Print on paper. $60 - $80

Disease comes from the mouth. Health education poster intended to reform food preparation practices. Jiangxi Province Shangyao area medical center. Print on paper. $60 - $80

少生优育
为子孙后代造福

经济繁荣 • 社会发达 • 资源丰富 • 环境优美 • 生活富裕 •••••

Fewer births provides higher quality education and creates a happier future for our children and grandchildren.
In small print, it reads "productive economy, resourceful, better environment and wealthier lifestyle." Tian
Junmin. Beijing Centre of Communication and Education for Family Planning. Print on paper. $80 - $120

Learn to Count (2). An educational poster, showing personal hygiene and dental care combined with a math lesson.
For use of 1st grade elementary school students. Tianjin People's publishing house. Print on paper. $50 - $70

小小牙齿用处大，　吃饭说话全靠它，
从小养成好习惯，　注意卫生保护牙。

保护牙齿挂图 1

陈永福 文　杨庆玲 画
北京市卫生教育所印制

Little teeth have a lot of usage, speaking and eating all depend on them, so make a good habit starting when you are young, pay attention to your hygiene and protect your health. Health education poster. Chen Yongfu and Yang Qingling. Beijing Health Educational Department. Print on paper. $60 - $80

欢迎你：

✚ 做一名红十字青少年

北京市红十字会印

Welcome you to become a Red Cross Youth. Beijing Red Cross Organization. Print on paper. $60 - $80

从小养成良好卫生习惯！

CONG XIAO YANG CHENG LIANG HAO WEI SHENG XI GUAN

Develop Good health habit from childhood. Feng Zengchun. Beijing Health and Immune Medical Center. Print on paper. $60 - $80

Eating more vegetables and whole grains will make the teeth strong and healthy, eat a varied diet, and teeth will be white and clean and healthy. Dental care educational wall poster #4. Print on paper. $60 - $80

Before a meal and after going to the bathroom, and before snacks, one must wash your hands. Yang Qingling. Beijing Health and Immune station and Beijing Health Educational Department. Print on paper. $60 - $80

Earthquake educational poster. Used at state-owned enterprises. Guangdong Revolution Committee Earthquake Office and Country Earthquake Guangzhou Earthquake Large Team. Print on paper. $60 - $80

In addition to being used in classrooms, these posters were sold at Xinhua bookstores for parents to buy, especially during the June 1st children's holiday. Parents often put them up in their children's rooms to encourage and promote good behavior.

Focus 3: Raising healthy, intelligent children.

As China entered into a relatively peaceful environment, traditional New Year posters featuring happy chubby babies, along with sayings for good luck, reappeared. In these posters, which had been popular in China for generations, one or more chubby babies hold good luck symbols and words such as "Every year is abundant" and "Happiness is coming." Typical symbols include carp, a symbol of wealth, and peaches, symbols of longevity. For years, Mao's image and words had replaced these traditional images. The reappearance of these reassuring images, with happy associations to past eras, helped the people to forget the chaotic Cultural Revolution, when traditional images had been forbidden, deemed to be part of the "four olds." The return of the traditional New Year decorations marked a shift in the political timbre of the country, to a time of relative tranquility in which the country could rebuild itself and families could start to heal their losses.

Caring. Zhou Enlai, Chinese premier, is seen surrounded by children of China. Used by Shanghai Education Department for 6th grade political education classes. Wang Guoliang. Print on paper. $60 - $80

节 节 高

Step by Step. Child playing with building blocks. Zhou Jianzhi. People's Art Publishing
House, July 1981. 210,000 copies. 0.13 Yuan. Print on paper. $50 - $70

我 帮 奶 奶 引 针 线

Helping Grandma Putting
Thread into the Needle. Liu
Zewen. People's Art Publishing
House, July 1982. 42,000
copies. 0.13 Yuan. Print on
paper. $60 - $80

划
龙
船

Riding the Dragon Boat. Zhu Xihuang. People's Sports Publishing House, August 1983.
1,380,000 copies. 0.16 Yuan. Print on paper. $60 - $80

Morning of a Holiday. Liu Guangcan.
Sichuan Publishing house, May 1982.
0.16 Yuan. Print on paper. $60 - $80

Pin Yin, Read and Write, six, seven, eight, nine and ten. Pin Yin is a system of Romanization of Chinese writing developed by the central government after 1949. Educational material for elementary school, late 1970s. Print on paper. $60 - $80

Write a play. Educational wall hanging poster – San Mao climbing to the moon. A comic character created by Zhang Leping from 1930s Shanghai, San Mao was a beggar who was adopted by a wealthy couple, but remained close to his roots and had a good heart. He later returned to his begging life. Late 1970s. Print on paper. $60 - $80

There was, however, some effort to incorporate China's political agenda into these traditional images. In addition to the chubby babies, posters began to appear with athletic images as the government sought to promote international athletic competition as a means to raise its international stature. The theme of modernization and material abundance also appeared to promote new policies, with depictions of high-rise buildings and consumer goods.

After Hua's two-year stint as the Chairman of the CCP, Deng Xiaoping took over the party leadership in 1978 and brought with him his two senior protégées, Hu Yaobang and Zhao Ziyang. Deng sought to build a "socialist country with Chinese characteristics."[8] He focused his efforts on modernization of four elements of the Chinese economy (agriculture, industry, national defense, and science & technology) and was given the title of the Chief Architect of the Chinese Economy by the Propaganda Department in 1992. The government published many propaganda posters during this period to mobilize and popularize the modernization effort. The Party emphasized the importance of the Chinese constitution (which was a very new thing, stress-

Focus 4: The ancient tradition

ing institutions over persons) and the Chinese national identity in an effort to move away from the cult of personality that ended so disastrously with Mao. This period represents the latest time from which items are scarce enough to make good collectibles. We do not cover later items in this book, but Dr. Stefan Landsberger's *Contemporary Chinese Propaganda Art* (http://www.iisg.nl/~landsberger/) is an excellent source for studying these later items.

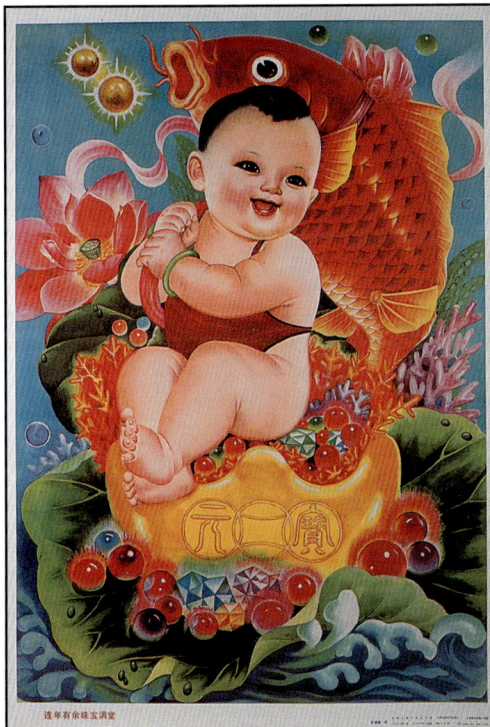

Golden Dragon playing with Spring Children. Zhu Xihuang. People's Sports Publishing House, August 1983. 0.20 Yuan. Print on paper. $70 - $90

Happy Baby Celebrate New Year. Liu Peiheng. Beijing Art and Photography Publishing house, November 1991. 0.60 Yuan. Print on paper. $60 - $80

Abundance for the year in and year out, and treasures are full in the house. Zhang Xuyuan. Jilin Art Publishing House, June 1991. 0.20 Yuan. Print on paper. $60 - $80

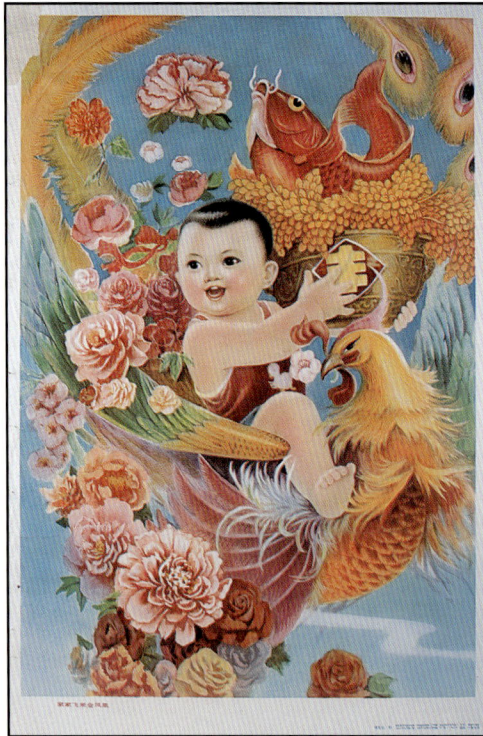

Golden phoenix is flying into everyone's home.
Zhen Jianshi. Hebei Art Publishing House, August
1983. 0.16 cents. Print on paper. $70 - $90

Happiness is abundant. Peng Haiqing. Tianjin
People's Publishing House, June 1988. 0.36 Yuan.
Print on paper. $70 - $90

Live is as long as the Southern Mountain. Child with peach (symbolizes longevity). Author Cheng Lizhi.
Tianjin Yangliuqing Art Publishing House, June 1991. 0.58 Yuan. Print on paper. $60 - $80

Rooster crows for Prosperity. Cheng Lizhi, author. Yangliuqing Art Publishing House, Tianjin, June 1992. Print on paper. $60 - $80

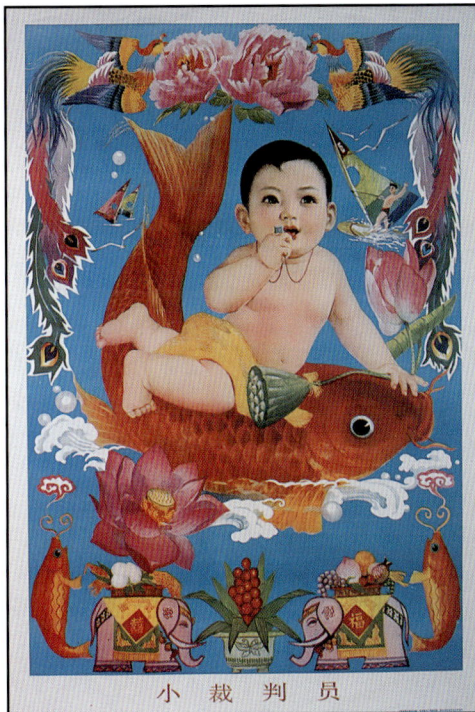

Little Judge. Author Chen Dongxiu. People's Sport Publishing House, August 1984. 0.16 Yuan. Print on paper. $70 - $90

Happiness is coming to the door. Cheng Lizhi. People's Fine Art Publishing House, June 1982. 1.5 million copies. 0.16 Yuan. Print on paper. $70 - $90

Dragon is flying and the Phoenix is dancing. Chen Zhenxin. People's Sports Publishing House, August 1984. 0.16 Yuan. Print on paper. $70 - $90

Golden Jade and Yearly Prosperity. Author Zhao Nansheng. Tianjin Yangliuqing Art Publishing House, June 1991. 0.58 Yuan. Print on paper. $60 - $80

172

All Nine Things are peaceful and with good fortune. Guo Qiming. Tianjin Yangliuqing Art Publishing House, June 1991. 0.58 Yuan. Print on paper. $60 - $80

Everything is to its satisfaction. No publishing or artist information available. Print on paper. $60 - $80

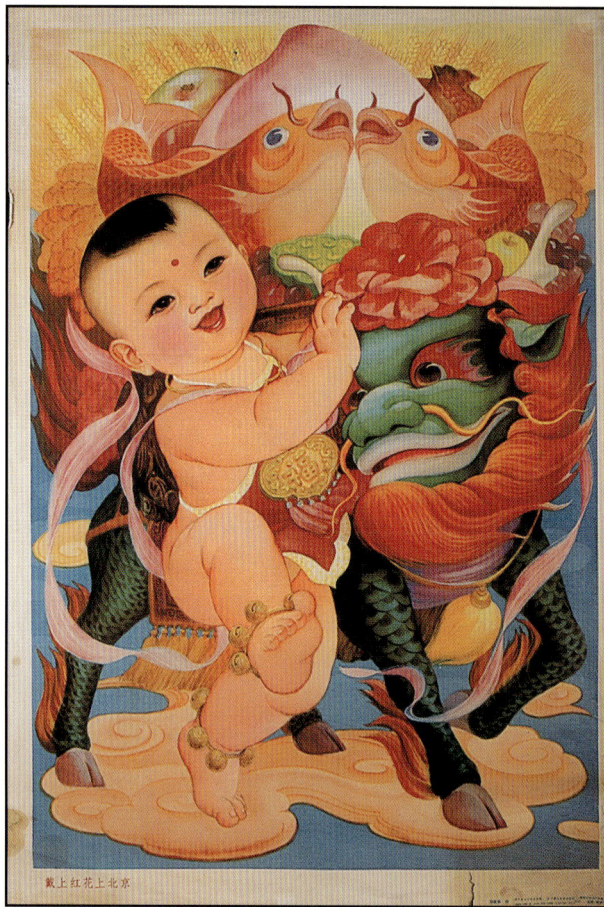

Bringing Red Flowers to Beijing. Liu Zhonglin. Liaoning Art Publishing House, July 1987. 0.20 Yuan. Print on paper. $60 - $80

Happiness, Luck and Everything to your Satisfaction. Author Ni Zhensheng. Tianjin Yangliuqing Art Publishing House, June 1985. 0.20 Yuan. Print on paper. $70 - $90

吉喜图

A picture of Luck and Happiness. Author Guo Jianguo. Shandong Art Publishing House, January 1984. 0.20 Yuan. Print on paper. $70 - $90

As you Wish. Author Li Zhifu. Tianjin Yangliuqing Art Publishing House, January 1991. 0.58 Yuan. Print on paper. $60 - $80

Luck and Happiness are abundant.
Author Sun Gongzhao. Agricultural
Reader's Publishing House, July 1988.
0.16 Yuan. Print on paper. $70 - $90

Harvesting Picture. Author by
Wang Lizhao. People's Art Publish-
ing House, February 1983. 0.20
Yuan. Print on paper. $70 - $90

Everything Changes in the Spring. Author Liu Zhongfu. People's Art Publishing House, June 1983. 0.20 Yuan. Print on paper. $70 - $90

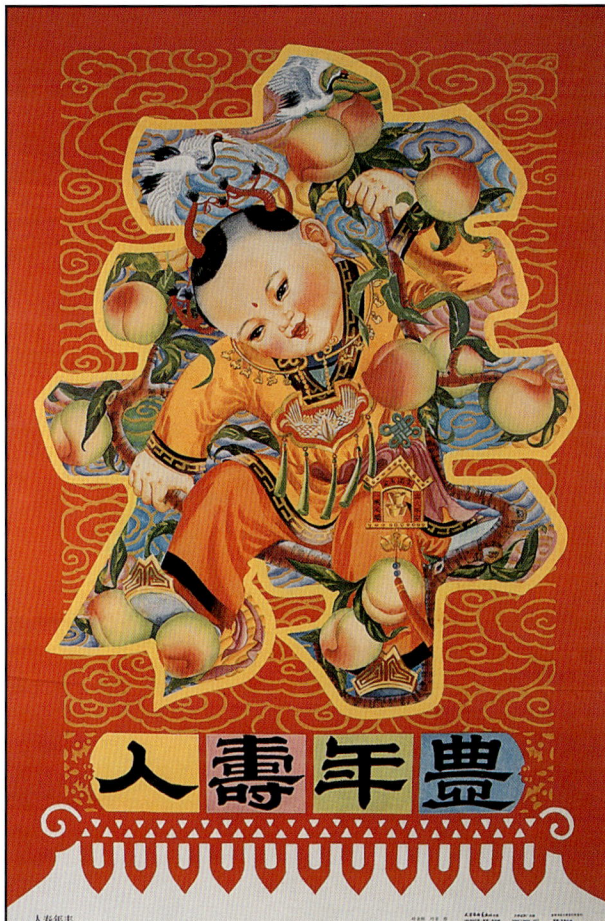

People enjoy longevity and The year enjoys a nice harvest. Authors Yi Yuhui and Yi Xin. Tianjin Yangliuqing Art Publishing House, June 1991. 0.58 Yuan. Print on paper. $60 - $80

Prosperity is Abundant. Authors Yi Yuhui and Yi Xin. Tianjin Yangliuqing Art Publishing House, June 1991. 0.58 Yuan. Print on paper. $60 - $80

Happiness is abundant. Authors Yi Yuhui and Yi Xin. Tianjin Yangliuqing Art Publishing House, June 1991. 0.58 Yuan. Print on paper. $60 - $80

Happiness and Prosperity are abundant. Author Li Shiyuan. Tianjin Yanjiu Publishing House, August 1988. 0.18 Yuan. Print on paper. $70 - $90

For the Country (praising the Chinese athletes). Author Dan Xihe. Tianjin Yangliuqing Art Publishing House, June 1985. 0.20 Yuan. Print on paper. $70 - $90

Colorful Phoenix Opening its Wings.
Author Wang Fantang. Shandong Art
Publishing House, May 1984. 0.18 Yuan.
Print on paper. $70 - $90

Congratulations on the New Double Happiness. Authors Chen Ying and Zhen Ming.
Tianjin Yangliuqing Art Publishing House,
1987. 0.58 Yuan. Print on paper. $70 - $90

百花迎新岁 彩灯映华年

Hundred flowers welcome the new year. Colorful lantern shines on a beautiful year. Chinese new year poster. Children holding a rocket. Print on paper. $60 - $80

Deng Xiaoping and Hu Yaobang reviewing the PLA army. mid 1980s. Ceramic flat panel wall hanging. $200 - $300

胡耀邦和邓小平在阅兵主席台上。

Focus 5: A socialist country with Chinese characteristics

A notable item from the early Deng period is included in this book, a ceramic wall plaque featuring a photo of Deng Xiaoping and Hu Yaobang. Hu, one of Deng's protégés and General Secretary of the Communist Party, was an active reformer who created a great deal of controversy within the party, most notably for failing to prevent demonstrations by students in 1986, resulting in his resignation in 1987. When Hu died in 1989, the resulting student demonstrations in Tiananmen Square grew into the Democracy movement that the government brutally crushed in June of that year. Although a beloved figure among students and political reformers, very little propaganda or official government items exist with Hu's image or words.

The challenge to the Communist Party that resulted from the Tiananmen Square incident and subsequent international condemnation resulted in a shift in the political climate back to an earlier, stricter time. The government reinstituted mandatory political study sessions and self-criticisms, repressing thoughts of democracy or freedom to ensure the Party's hold on the country in the late 1980s and early 1990s.

Our Flag is Communism. Author Wang Hui. Beijing Publishing House. 0.16 Yuan. Print on paper. $70 - $90

Our Flag is Communism. Created to celebrate the 12th Chinese Communist Party Representative Meeting. Author Qiu Baiping. People's Art Publishing House, August 1982. 0.16 Yuan. Print on paper. $70 - $90

China belongs to the Chinese People. Elementary school educational material in commemoration of the creation of the Chinese constitution. Depicts peasant, factory worker, PLA soldier, and ethnic minorities. Author Qiu Runmin. Shanghai Educational Publishing House. Print on paper. $70 - $90

Chapter 10
Ceramic Statues

In recent years a large number of ceramic statues and figures have appeared in flea markets and shops in large cities across China. They typically depict political figures, characters or scenes from popular Peking Operas and ballets (especially those popular during the Cultural Revolution), and characters from propaganda campaigns, such as Lei Feng. Prior to 1966, color ceramic and porcelain statues primarily featured central government leaders such as Mao, Zhou and model citizens and heroes such as Wang Jinxi (model factory worker) and Chen Yonggui (model farmer). Artists and designers employed by government-owned agencies throughout the country, known as Ceramic and Porcelain Research Centers, would jointly work with art academy graduates. In 1963 and 1964, more ceramic statues were produced to support a shift in the political climate toward class struggle. Statues depicting vicious landowners being "struggled against" by the people, in both clay and ceramic format, were common. Also common were statues featuring people holding guns pointed at other political criminals, who were draped with white boards indicating their political crimes such as "country sell out" (traitor) or "spy."

By the beginning of 1966, with the introduction of Modern Revolutionary Peking operas and ballets, a number of characters originating from these plays were made, often depicting a famous scene from the operas and ballets. These statues were made to be memorabilia items or keepsakes, and were not typically sold. They were often given to Mao's Thoughts Propaganda Team members. Like the pins, they were hot memorabilia items at the time and everyone would want to own one. In addition, some of those who had been placed in the "Stinking 9th Category", technicians and artists, would create these struggle-themed sculptures upon their release from prison, putting themselves in as the target as a way to reform themselves by self-criticism. The figures would also be used to commemorate significant events in Chinese history. Mao and Lin reviewing the Cultural Revolution Red Guards army was a familiar and popular image, and thus a statue was created to copy a photograph or poster image of this event. Mao swimming in the Yangzi and mingling with the people was another famous image and this was also captured in a statue. Unlike other factories which had their production work halted due to the study of Mao's Thoughts, ceramic factories had more than enough work to keep them running year-round.

Every ceramic factory would strive to create new and popular designs, competing against its peers. The Revolutionary Committees would also commission statues to mark significant dates and events, and distribute them to important members, often at banquets held to mark the occasion. At one point Mao criticized the use of scarce metal to make buttons and bronze items, and therefore ceramics were considered a more appropriate medium for political plaques, statue, and other items.

After the Cultural Revolution, many of the central controls on the economy began to loosen, along with central support of state-owned enterprises. As a result, many of the ceramic factories began to close as they lost their patrons, and the workers in those factories began to make ceramic figures in their homes or private kilns and sell them in the small village markets that had begun to grow after the agricultural reforms instituted by Deng. This happened mainly in Konglin and Zhuzhou, Hunan Province; Jingdezhen in Jiangxi Province, and Tangshan in Hebei Province. Since many peasants were illiterate and not up to date with current political doctrines, they sometimes made statues, such as Lin Biao, that were not politically acceptable. By the mid 1980s, the economy has diversified somewhat and many of these workers found other, more lucrative, ways to make a living. The privately made ceramic figures are very rare – on frequent trips to China we have very seldom seen them.

In the early 1990s, the Chinese government issued regulations prohibiting materials from the Cultural Revolution. Like many other prohibitions, the restriction on selling Cultural Revolution items only increased their price and therefore encouraged procurement and sales. With the increasing interest from the Western world, business people who saw opportunities started to gather Cultural Revolution artifacts from the countryside and brought them to markets in major cities. In the late 1990s, in fact, individuals began to find the old casts and equipment used to make the original statues and produce them again. Because the production is very labor intensive, and because in many cases it is impossible to tell an original from a reproduction cast more recently with the same equipment, reproductions and original items fetch similar prices in Chinese markets. In addition, the original items are recent enough that there are many still available in excellent condition, appearing to be essentially new.

Chapter 11
Price Guide

The prices in the photo captions, where indicated, are the prices for the items when they were published or produced. The market for Chinese political memorabilia is in its infancy in the West, and the demand from American and European collectors has resulted in significant price increases, even in local Chinese markets. With these price increases has come a rash of reproductions and fakes, typical for China. The fakes are usually quite convincing, and condition is seldom a good indicator of an item's authenticity.[9] As with all historical items, *caveat emptor* applies.

Posters: The price for posters varies widely. At retail from dealers in the United States and Europe the price ranges from $20-$600 per poster, depending on condition, rarity and desirability. The most popular posters are those associated with well-known events, such as the Cultural Revolution or the Great Leap Forward, and campaigns, such as anti-imperialism or the one-child policy.

As with many items in China, reproductions abound and are typically represented as original. At flea markets and other venues in China, the prices are quite variable and subject to negotiation. Furthermore, there does not appear to be much distinction in price between originals and reproductions. Although it is always difficult to confirm authenticity, the material, condition and markings on a poster are good guides. Posters produced during the Cultural Revolution were usually produced on very thin paper, and typically provide information in the lower right corner about the posters' publication and source. Without knowledge of written Chinese, however, it is difficult to discern the meaning of these marks. There are exceptions to these rules, however. Some of the posters produced to be double sided and put on a propaganda board or on the street in a glass case were made of thicker material, and some posters were made without publication marks. The best course of action, especially for the beginning collector, is to educate oneself and understand the subject matter of the items.

Ceramic Items: expect to pay from $10 - $300 for ceramic ware. The price varies mainly with size, ranging from a tiny pen holder to a huge vase, up to 36 inches tall, with an image of Mao and revolutionary slogans. As with other memorabilia, the authenticity of items is very difficult to determine. Both original and copies are typically made crudely, and the condition of both can vary widely. For some reason many of the current reproductions are stamped with the year 1968.

Ceramic Statues: Color ceramic statues can range from $30 to $300 at retail (and sometimes more for particularly rare items). The size and complexity vary widely, from simple single figures to large compositions composed of six or seven figures with many details. Single statues are at the bottom of this range, from $30 to $70, and double figurine statues range from $70 to $130. The more complex figures sell at prices above this, up to $300 or so.

Metal Figurines: Mao busts and figures range in price from $30 to $200, depending on condition, size and complexity.

Red Books: Red Books were produced in astounding numbers throughout the Cultural Revolution and in many editions, and continue to be produced today as souvenirs.[10] New Red Books and older ones of no distinguishing characteristics sell for minimal prices, ranging from $10 to $30. Very early editions from 1964, with a paper cover rather than in plastic and in reasonable condition, can fetch anywhere from $50 to $200. The prices for later Red Books depend a great deal on the rarity of the particular edition and the presence of other factors, such as handwritten notes or identifying information, or additional items, such as ration coupons, train tickets or visitation badges secreted inside or used as bookmarks, or Red Books that either have Lin Biao's photo and calligraphy intact or torn out. There are also Red Books devoted to the Thoughts of Vice-Chairman Lin Biao, created essentially in competition with Mao Zedong Thought.[11] These books bring $40 to $100 retail, but can be more. Red Books featuring the Gang of Four are both relatively rare and of particular historical interest, and thus often command premium prices.

Ration tickets: These items are relatively abundant and typically sell at low price points, $2 or less each, often much less.

Pins and buttons: Pins and buttons are also quite common, but are a particularly collectible item across many types of memorabilia, including items from the Cultural Revolutions, and therefore often sell at or above $10.

Appendix 1
Cultural RevolutionTimeline

Time	Name	Brief description
1949-1951	Land Reform	The land reform process was called *fanshen*, "overturning of the body." Communal meals were offered to poor peasants. Landlords and errant party members were brought before citizen's councils for criticism and punishment. Land holdings of larger landlords distributed to the people.
1950 - 1953	Support North Koreans in the Korean War	Mao Zedong orders the Chinese People's Volunteers to march into North Korea and fight in the Korean War. The Ceasefire Agreement was signed on July 27, 1953, effectively ending the Korean War.
1950 - 1953	Suppressing Counter-revolutionary Activities Campaign	Campaign aimed at eliminating any remaining counterrevolutionary Nationalist Party members. 4.7 million people are estimated to have died during this campaign.
1952	Fight the Three Evils and Five Evils Campaign	The Three Evils consisted of corruption, waste and bureaucracy. The five evils were characterized as qualities of capitalists and corrupt officials, and included bribery, tax evasion, theft of state-owned property, cheating in contracts with the government, and stealing economic information.
1953	Agricultural Collectivization	Campaign to form agricultural collectives along the lines of the Soviet model, taking back control of land distributed to farmers during the land reform movement.
1954–1955	Socialist Enterprise and Business Reform	Government aimed to buy back companies and industries from private owners. In fact, very little funding was available for this effort and private owners received pennies on the dollar, at best. The campaign resulted in transfer of virtually all private business assets to state-controlled enterprises.
1955	Hu Feng Event and Campaign against counter-revolutionary bourgeois idealism	Hu Feng, a left-wing Shanghainese writer from the 1930s, was criticized for his views on literature and art. Mao Zedong wrote a long article, criticizing him and other intellectuals as "down-right bourgeois idealists and against the Party and the people".

1956	Hundred Flowers Campaign	Director of the Propaganda Department of the Chinese Communist Party (CCP) Lu Dingyi makes a speech titled "Let a hundred flowers bloom; let a hundred schools of thought contend", which starts a new policy of openness in literature and art.
1957	Anti Rightist Movement	Started out as calling people to help the CCP by providing suggestions and criticism, it ended with the Anti Rightist Campaign, whereby half a million intellectuals were labeled "Rightists," often based on statements made during the Hundred Flowers Campaign. After the Cultural Revolution, all but 8 people were rectified.
1958	The Great Leap Forward	Commonly referred as the Steel Campaign. The Second Session of the Eighth National Congress proposed to change China's backward economic and cultural conditions as quickly as possible. Mao Zedong claimed that China could catch up with Great Britain in seven years and the United States in fifteen by means of a "great leap forward." Instruments made of iron were donated to be made into steel in backyard smelters, but instead ended up as pig iron.
1959-1961	Famine	Hunger and malnutrition resulted in a death toll exceeding 40 million between 1959 and 1961. The starvation came about from three main factors, natural disasters; the Great Leap Forward, during which agricultural output stalled; and worsened Sino-Soviet relations, which resulted in reduced Soviet grain imports.
1959	Lushan Meeting	The Politburo held an enlarged meeting in Lushan. During this meeting, Marshal Peng Dehuai voiced his criticism of the Great Leap Forward and was removed from his position as Defense Minister.
1962	Beginning of Class Struggle Sessions	During the Tenth Session of the Eighth CPC Central Committee, Mao Zedong states that class struggle must be stressed every year, every month, and every day. Mao's thoughts during this meeting were implemented and led to class struggle meetings

		throughout China.	ment of the CCP Central Committee, which enables him to rehabilitate and rectify wrongs committed during the Cultural Revolution. During the Third Plenary Session of the Eleventh Central Committee of the CCP, the policies and practices of Cultural Revolution are formally renounced and class struggle is no longer a focus of the government. Economic reform and progress becomes the new emphasis for the Chinese government. Deng tells the Chinese people that "to get rich is glorious."
1963-1965	Socialist Education Campaign	Mao Zedong calls a meeting of the Politburo to strengthen the Socialist Education Campaign in rural areas. He calls for a mass movement to repulse the capitalist and feudal forces.	
1966 – 1976	The Great Proletarian Cultural Revolution	The Cultural Revolution Group of the Politburo is established, with Chen Boda as its director and including as members Kang Sheng, Jiang Qing, and Zhang Chunqiao. The Cultural Revolution formally starts. Mao Zedong dies on September 9, 1976. On October 6, 1976, members of the Gang of Four are arrested. Cultural Revolution comes to an end.	
1978	Opening to the outside world and economic reform	Deng Xiaoping is reinstated to his position as vice-chairman of the Party Central Committee at the Third Plenary Session of the Eleventh Central Committee of the CCP. College entry exams and university enrollment resume. Hu Yaobang is appointed director of the Propaganda Depart-	

Appendix 2
Revolution Model Plays

The White-Haired Girl

Type: *Modern Revolutionary Ballet*

Major Characters: Xi Er, the white-haired girl. *Da Chun*, her fiancé *Yang Bailao*, Xi Er's father. *Mu Renzhi*, abusive landowner, Nationalist Party traitor. *Huang Shiren*, abusive landowner.

Synopsis: Prior to the liberation of 1949, landowner *Huang Shiren* abused and enslaved his tenants. A poor peasant named *Yang Bailao* couldn't repay the debt owed to *Huang* and committed suicide on Chinese New Year's Eve. *Xi Er*, afraid of being enslaved by *Huang*, escapes to the wilderness and subsists on plant roots and anything else she finds. Her hair turns completely white from malnutrition and worry. Her fiancé joins the People's Liberation Army, and brings the army to his village, rescuing the villagers and Xi Er from the abusive landowner.

The Red Army Detachment of Women

Type: *Modern Revolutionary Ballet*

Major Characters: *Wu Qinghua*, female soldier. *Hong Changqing*, Chinese Communist Party (CCP) Representative. *Nan Batian*, abusive landowner.

Synopsis: During the Sino-Japanese war (1937 – 1945), a detachment of female soldiers from Hainan Island fights the Japanese invaders. *Wu Qinghua* is a servant in a landowner's home who suffers abuse and harassment at the hands of her master. She escapes and meets CCP representative Hong Changqing, who recruits her into the Red Army. She leads a Red Army detachment of women soldiers, finds the abusive landowner *Nan Batian* and defeats him and his henchmen, saving his victims in the process.

Sha Jia Bang

Type: Modern Revolutionary Peking Opera

Major Characters: *Guo Jianguang*, New Fourth Army commander. *A Qing Sao*, Auntie *A Qing*, a tea shop owner and underground CCP member. *Diao Deyi*, lieutenant and Nationalist Party member. *Hu Chunkui*, Captain, Nationalist Party member.

Synopsis: During the Sino-Japanese war, the commander of the New Fourth Army, *Guo Jianguang*, brings eight wounded soldiers to rest and recover at *Sha Jia Bang*. Underground CCP member *A Qing Sao* shelters them in her tea shop, hiding them from the Nationalists. The Red Army soldiers recover and return to the battlefield victorious.

The Red Lantern

Type: Modern Revolutionary Peking Opera

Major Characters: *Li Yuhe*, underground CCP member and railroad worker. *Li Tiemei*, daughter of martyr adopted by *Li Yuhe. Jiu Shan*: Japanese Army captain.

Synopsis: During the Sino-Japanese war, CCP member Liu Yuhe, his daughter Li Tiemei and the people around them work underground for the CCP. As part of a guerilla resistance force they resist the Japanese invaders.

Raid on the White Tiger Regiment

Type: Modern Revolutionary Peking Opera

Major Characters: *Yan Weicai*, Chinese People's Volunteer Force scout.

Synopsis: During the "War to resist America and Aid Korea", a Chinese People's Volunteer Force scouting division, lead by *Yan Weicai* probe deep into enemy territory undetected and destroy an enemy command post.

On the Docks

Type: Modern Revolutionary Peking Opera

Major Characters: *Fang Haizhen*, secretary of the CCP.

Synopsis: Shanghai dock workers strive to ensure the quality of their work. Secretary of the CCP Fang Haizhen leads her team to perform quality control on every shipment, despite the pressures of many packages and little time. They are able to find missing packages and ensure that the shipments proceed without delay.

The Song of Praise of Long Jiang

Type: Modern Revolutionary Peking Opera

Major Characters: *Jiang Shuiying*: female lead, secretary of the CCP for the village

Synopsis: When a flood is about to engulf the village, the secretary of the CCP Jiang Shuiying leads the

Endnotes

people to fight the flood and achieve success.

Taking Tiger Mountain by Strategy
Type: Modern Revolutionary Peking Opera
Major Characters: *Yang Zirong*, scout platoon leader in the PLA*Shao Jianbo*, chief of staff in the PLA.*Zuo Shangdiao*, commander of the Nationalist Party Army

Synopsis: Borrowing the story of *Tracks in the Snowy Forest*, the story describes how *Yang Zirong* bravely infiltrates the Tiger Mountain (*Wei Hu Shan*) stronghold of the Nationalist Party Army in northeast China during the Chinese Civil War. He gains the trust of the commander of the Nationalist forces and obtains intelligence that allows the PLA to destroy the Nationalist Party Army, and liberate the people of Tiger Mountain.

Du Juan Shan
Type: Modern Revolutionary Peking Opera
Major Characters: *Ke Xiang*, CCP Representative.*Lei Gang*, guerrilla leader.

Synopsis: During the Sino-Japanese war, a guerrilla team residing in the mountains finds itself unable to fight the Japanese successfully, in part due to internal tensions stemming from class differences. Under the guidance of the CCP representative *Ke Xiang*, the guerrilla force sets their differences aside, and puts the conflict with Japanese invaders before class differences. The guerrilla force unites and gains victory over the Japanese army.

[1] The character in this case refers to Chinese writing, which consists of ideograms/pictograms rather than letters and words.

[2] Although the poster did not name them, this was understood in the context of the time

[3] This brought about some disastrous results, including rural collectivization that led to mass starvation and, arguably, the Great Leap Forward that caused the deaths of tens of millions.

[4] To be fair, in the long run productivity increases obtain exactly this result.

[5] Here the government had arguably followed a Soviet policy that was not appropriate for Chinese conditions. In the USSR, the collectivization of agriculture allowed for economies of scale, in theory, through the purchase of mechanized equipment and other factors. China did not have those possibilities, and collectivization resulted only in larger groups working on larger fields, with a removal of the connection between the labor of an individual farmer and his benefit.

[6] This applies to windup watches. Digital quartz watches, of course, are of more recent origin.

[7] The rationed goods included items as diverse as meat, gasoline, fabric, animal fodder, cotton, cooking oil, vinegar, soy sauce, salt and sugar

[8] Although presented as a modernization campaign, some understood it to signal the introduction of market mechanisms into the Chinese economy.

[9] Because many items have been produced within the past few decades, and in some cases have been stored, they can be in almost new condition. On the other hand, many scuffed or worn items can be new but treated to look that way.

[10] Different versions of the Red Book were produced by factory and political units at the time. Though Red Books as souvenirs are mostly in English and are only published by the Chinese Foreign Languages Press.

[11] As noted above, Red Books often served to store important documents and for taking down notes

Bibliography

Gao, Wenqian. *Later Years of Zhou Enlai (Wan Nian Zhou Enlai)*. Ming Jing Publishing, 2003

Heng, Liang and Judith Shapiro. *Son of the Revolution.* New York: Vintage Books, 1984.

Yan Jiaqi and Gao Gao. *Turbulent Decade – A History of the Cultural Revolution.* Honolulu: University of Hawai'i Press, 1996.

Feng Jicai. *Ten Years of Madness – Oral Histories of China's Cultural Revolution.* San Francisco: China Books, 1996.

Kaplan, Frederic M., Julian M. Sobin and Stephen Andors. *Encyclopedia of China Today.* Harper & Row, New York, 1979.

Landsberger, Stefan. *Chinese Propaganda Posters.* Amsterdam: The Pepin Press, 1995.

Li, Zhensheng. *Red-Color News Soldier.* London: Phaidon Press, 2003.

MacFarquhar, Roderick. *The Origins of the Cultural Revolution 3: The Coming of the Cataclysm 1961-1966.* New York: Columbia University Press, 1997.

_____. *The Origins of the Cultural Revolution 1: Contradictions Among the People 1956-1957.* New York: Columbia University Press, 1974.

_____. *The Origins of the Cultural Revolution 2: The Great Leap Forward 1958-1960.* New York: Columbia University Press, 1983.

MacFarquhar, Roderick (ed.). *The Politics of China.* Cambridge, England: Cambridge University Press, 1997.

Schoenhals, Michael (ed.). *China's Cultural Revolution, 1966-1969 – Not a Dinner Party.* Armonk: M.E. Sharpe, 1996.

Schrift, Melissa. *Biography of a Chairman Mao Badge – the Creation and Mass Consumption of a Personality Cult.* New Brunswick: Rutgers University Press, 2001.

Schurmann, Frank and Orville Schell. *The China Reader: Communist China.* New York: Random House, 1967).

Twitchett, Denis, and John K. Fairbank (eds.). *The Cambridge History of China: Volume 14.* New York: Cambridge University Press, 1987.

_____. *The Cambridge History of China: Volume 15.* New York: Cambridge University Press, 1991.

Wolf, Michael. *Chinese Propaganda Posters.* Cologne: Taschen, 2003.

Yuan, Gao. *Born Red – A Chronicle of the Cultural Revolution.* Stanford: Stanford University Press, 1987.

Zhai Zhenhua. *Red Flower of China.* New York: Soho Press, 1992.

Zhong, Xueping, Wang Zheng, and Bai Di. *Some of Us.* New Brunswick, NJ: Rutgers University Press, 2001.

Index